# Home-Based Newsletter Publishing

# Also by William J. Bond

*Home-Based Mail Order: A Success Guide for Entrepreneurs*
  (Liberty Hall Press/McGraw-Hill)

# Home-Based Newsletter Publishing

## A Success Guide for Entrepreneurs

*William J. Bond*

**McGraw-Hill, Inc.**
New York   St. Louis   San Francisco   Auckland   Bogotá
Caracas   Lisbon   London   Madrid   Mexico   Milan
Montreal   New Delhi   Paris   San Juan   Singapore
Sydney   Tokyo   Toronto

**To my late sister Gail Bond Sine, and to my late
brother Joseph "Jock" Bond. May God be with
you both.**

Library of Congress Cataloging-in-Publication Data: 91-067601

3 4 5 6 7 8 9 0   DOH DOH 9 7 6 5 4 3 2

ISBN   0-07-006556-X
ISBN   0-07-006557-8   {PBK}

*The sponsoring editor for this book was David Conti, the editing supervisors were
Caroline Levine and Ruth Mannino, and the production supervisor was Donald
F. Schmidt. It was set in Garamond Light by McGraw-Hill's Professional Book
Group composition unit.*

*Printed and bound by R. R. Donnelley & Sons Company.*

This publication is designed to provide accurate and authoritative information in re-
gard to the subject matter covered. It is sold with the understanding that the publisher
is not engaged in rendering legal, accounting or other professional service. If legal advice or other expert assistance is required, the services of a competent professional
person should be sought.
*—from a declaration of principles jointly adopted by a committee
of the American Bar Association and a committee of publishers*

# Contents

# Preface

The information age is here. People will pay for information simply because they lack the time or knowledge to get it themselves. You can start a home-based newsletter and earn excellent money by filling information needs.

How much money can you earn? This depends on your newsletter topic and on following the step-by-step directions outlined in this book. Many newsletter owners earn excellent money working right out of their homes—no work commute, no stress from a difficult boss, and no office politics.

Success in newsletter publishing is measured not only in terms of the money you will earn. You will gain a reputation as a leader in your particular field. An engineer in Massachusetts owns a monthly newsletter entitled *The Energy Report & Analysis*, which is sold all over the country to people interested in new hard-to-get energy information. This energy newsletter is a successful business, and the owner is gaining a national reputation.

This book will help you start your business quickly, and will give you all the information necessary to make your business a success. You will learn how to choose a winning topic, and decide on the best title. You will discover how to choose the best newsletter articles, and whether to advocate, dissent, or remain objective in your newsletter approach. You will learn how to design your newsletter. You will learn how to research, write, edit, and proofread with speed and accuracy. You will learn how to choose the right people to help you with writing and production. And you will learn the shortcuts to excellent printing and newsletter distribution.

This book shows you how to get *free* publicity, and how to get subscribers to renew year after year. You can learn how to do your marketing plan, and how to manage your business from taxes, to copyrights, to customer service techniques. *Home-Based Newsletter Publishing* covers all you need to be successful in this exciting field.

*William J. Bond*

# Home-Based Newsletter Publishing

# 1

# Setting up your home-based business

Congratulations! You deserve special recognition. You have purchased a book to explore the numerous opportunities, challenges, and profits available in the home-based world of newsletter publishing. You not only can earn money, but you might conceivably become known nationally, or internationally. This book, *Home-Based Newsletter Publishing,* will give you the information essential to make your dream come true.

One of the questions I often hear in my newsletter seminars is, "What's the difference between a newsletter for subscribers, and a nonprofit newsletter for club or association members, a school, or a hospital, which you simply distribute free of charge?" In this book I will focus on the steps necessary to make a newsletter the best possible for total readership satisfaction, whether it's intended for subscribers or for members of an association. A quality, finely tuned newsletter with a sharp focus will be the primary goal of this book. Your quality newsletter will give you renewals year after year. Even if your initial intent is to publish for nonsubscribers, read all the chapters thoroughly, as though you were planning to sell to subscribers, and you'll be armed with all the information you need to succeed in any newsletter-publishing endeavor.

A newsletter is, by definition, a self-covered periodical, normally 4 to 16 pages long, which carries news, without advertising, aimed at a special audience. It may be issued in any frequency, but is most commonly published monthly. It appeals to audiences of any size—subscriptions lists can run from a few hundred to hundreds of thousands—and may cost anywhere from $6 to $2,000 annually. A newsletter can make you rich. Let's say you sell your newsletter for $59 per year to 1500 subscribers; your gross revenue will be $88,500! You can become very well known. This book will show you how to build on your new visibility and turn it into other opportunities.

## What are the secrets to success?

The newsletter business is like any other business in that it requires a strong interest in and knowledge of the business. The newsletter subject, whether it's raising race horses, consulting, pets, or nuclear energy, must be something you enjoy and can discuss with interest and enthusiasm day after day, month after month—almost endlessly. If you find it difficult to hide your enthusiasm, interest, or knowledge of your newsletter subject, your customers will notice it. Your energy and enthusiasm are important keys to your success.

Another key to success is choosing a subject, and then delivering a publication that fills the customers' needs. For example, a newsletter owner in New Hampshire decided to publish a newsletter on consulting. His newsletter focused on trends in and news of the field, and discussed candidly practitioners who were not doing business ethically. He became the watchdog of the consulting field. He used his skills, interests, experience, and knowledge to give him a special platform to deliver an excellent product.

## What equipment is necessary?

Very little. All you need is a typewriter, either manual or electric, or a typist to handle the typing for you. A printer can print up your newsletters. Many newsletter owners are using computers to produce their newsletters. We will discuss this in more detail later in the book.

## Newsletter publishing is a natural home business

You can start the business from the comfort of your den or basement home office. You do not have to sign an expensive, multiyear lease for an expensive office in a congested city to start your business. The newsletter business opens the door to the best of two worlds: being your own boss, and being able to start up and run your own business right in your home. Another important feature to this business is ease of distribution of the product; the United States Postal Service will deliver your newsletter all over the country. You will not be required to place your product in expensive retail stores or in catalogs; you can sell and distribute your newsletter to anyone who receives postal service, anywhere in the world.

## You sell information

You are important to your readers. You fill a need by giving them important information that is not available elsewhere. For example, one successful newsletter owner used his interest in and knowledge of recycling to sell subscriptions to both individuals and entire towns and cities. This newsletter included the latest news on recycling, laws relating to recycling, and planning and marketing of recycling products. An important segment of the market for the newsletter was towns and cities without an ongoing recycling program. The strategy of the publisher was to keep the subscribers abreast of the most advanced recycling techniques, and to provide success stories of successful programs.

Or take the example of a New Hampshire newsletter owner, who started a newsletter on computers right at home, just when the trend toward use of computers started in the United States. The owner put out a 12-page monthly publication filled with important information on how to use computers successfully. The subscribers enjoyed it, and the subscription list grew and grew. Once again, all the writing was done in the den of the owner's home. As success increased, competitors arrived to try to wrestle away part of the business. The owner stood tall and continued to produce a quality newsletter. One by one, the competitors faded into the night. This newsletter became so successful, it was sold as a magazine to a large publishing house. Today's successful newsletter may become tomorrow's successful magazine!

A third prospective newsletter owner was interested in career opportunities for American women. This exciting newsletter was started in the Pennsylvania home of a publisher who worked as a full-time administrator during the day. The focus of this newsletter became careers for women in the information field; it has a mission of showing where the jobs are today, and what jobs will be available in the future.

Yet another success story is the woman from Illinois who decided she would start a newsletter to help salespeople sell more products and services by giving them new ideas and techniques. An important part of this newsletter was its positive and inspirational tone. It kept its subscribers selling successfully. This publisher ran her newsletter at home, and worked as a secretary during the day. She spent her free time researching sales trends at her local and community college libraries, and interviewed salespeople for important information. This newsletter was started by offering the potential subscribers a free trial period for 30 days; this gave the owner an opportunity to offer her best possible product, so the subscriber could purchase it.

One successful entrepreneur from Washington turned his sales experience and interest in writing into a winning newsletter for writers. His newsletter, based on his own experience, gives his customers information on earning a steady income by setting up a home-based business. His newsletter subscribers are in many different businesses, for example, automobiles, mail order, construction, finance, consulting, and real estate. This entrepreneur is wealthy because he saw an important need for information by a specific market group, and then delivered products and services to meet it. This book will help you do the same thing.

## How do you get the information?

Good question. This is the most popular question at my newsletter seminars. Information is the most important service you provide to your readers. You offer the best, most up-to-date, difficult-to-find information available. You get information from many sources including magazines, newspapers, trade magazines, newsletters, books, and personal contacts. Just as newspaper reporters have sources to get the latest information, your sources can be the people you know in a particular industry or field. For example, a newsletter owner from New Jersey, who writes on small business operations, has as one of her key contacts the executive director of a small business association serving various businesses in New Jersey and Pennsylvania. Your success in this business will depend on your ability to get the right information at the right time. Be persistent and follow up on any leads.

You will develop information from three basic sources: direct observation, interviews with key contacts such as the above, and secondary material, such as books, reports, documents, and references, which can be found in your public library. For example, a newsletter owner whose subject is the rights of the elderly must go beyond books and newspaper articles, by observing the elderly shopping for food, clothing, and medical services and visiting the elderly in nursing homes, homeless shelters, and retirement communities. The newsletter becomes alive and vibrant when the writer meets the subjects directly, gets to know them, and keeps learning more about them. A successful newsletter owner is a continual learner.

## Your right to publish

Freedom of the press, in the words of the Continental Congress of 1774, establishes "the advancement of truth, science, morality, and the arts in general" and the maintenance of "honorable and just modes of conducting public affairs." Many important statespeople have fought hard for freedom of expression, time after time standing up to be counted. Your right to publish is protected by the U.S. Constitution. You are protected to say what you want, as long as it is not slanderous and is the truth, based on your experience and research. You are empowered to share your knowledge, information, and ideas.

## Setting up your home office

People who start a newsletter set up an office, or at least a place to work, to get the essential work done. This is not necessarily a separate room or area in your home or apartment; it might be a small area in a room, or a section of your basement or attic. Choose a separate area, preferably one away from the noisy part of your house, where you can concentrate on doing your writing and research. When planning to set up your office, you must address three important questions: What is the problem? When should you set up your office? Where should you locate your office? Let's review each question.

1. *What is the problem?*   You live in a house or apartment and, for the most part, your activities are personal in nature. Now you want to start a home-based newsletter business, and it will require discipline, persistence, and action to succeed. You must begin to see yourself as a successful newsletter owner and then act to move in the direction of success. For example, Stan in New Hampshire works at a bank in collections, and wants to start a newsletter for collection managers. In reviewing his apartment, he decides to use a corner of the bedroom for his office, so that he can close the door to avoid the noise from the television, VCR, and stereo. Stan decides to spend at least an hour a day in his office either writing or researching for future issues of his newsletter. Stan also plans to visit the local business library to get information on his newsletter subject area. Stan expects to send his first issue out about two months after he sets up his office.

2. *When should you set up your office?*   As soon as possible! Determine a time frame for your first newsletter, and then plan to set up your office. For example, Mary, a teacher from Indiana, wants to start a newsletter for parents of handicapped children. Mary plans to set up her office in May, so that it will be ready by the start of her summer vacation in June, and she schedules her first issue for August or September. Set up your office sufficiently in advance of the date you decide to publish your first issue. Start to gather information, and put it into a separate file. Take the time necessary to set up an office at home, and then give yourself enough quality time to produce results that will gain you a reputation and a following.

3. *Where should you locate your office?*   In two words: somewhere quiet. In my college seminars, I ask students to choose a room in a quiet and separate, if possible, portion of their apartment, condominium, or house for their newsletter busi-

ness. One of my students was renting a small room without space for the desk and files necessary for a newsletter business. He decided to rent a larger room that could accommodate a desk, chair, file cabinet, books, and publications.

There are many options for office location. Another student started a newsletter on veterans' benefits. She located her office in her basement next to the washing machine and dryer. It was very difficult to concentrate, so she moved to the other end of the basement to avoid the noise. Be willing to move your office until you get a location that works for you.

A successful Maine newsletter owner set up an office in a garage at the back of his house. The garage had sufficient room for the books, magazines, and files necessary for his research. His newsletter, which helps retailers sell more merchandise, has a national subscription base and is growing each day.

## Success requires your time

Someone once said that success only comes before work in the dictionary. This is true in the newsletter business; it requires time and effort to choose the best topic, and once chosen, to turn out quality newsletters issue after issue. Some time each day should be allocated for your newsletter; you might read magazines or books, review new subscriber lists, or write a sales letter for new subscribers. Be willing to spend the time necessary to be successful.

## Select a business organization for your needs

There are several types of business organization setups for you to choose from. The *sole proprietorship* is when you supply all the money necessary to get started, and you also are credited with all income and losses. The advantage to the sole proprietorship is that you can get started quickly without excessive paperwork, but the drawback is you are personally liable for the business losses and other business liabilities.

Some newsletter owners set up a *partnership*. For example, a writer will make an agreement with a researcher to start a newsletter, and each partner contributes expertise and capital to the business. A partnership is an agreement by two or more people that must be in writing, and should be drawn up by an attorney. The contract should include the partners' names, addresses, duties in business, and investments in the partnership as well as an agreement as to how losses and profits will be shared and how the business can be terminated. Partnerships also have personal liabilities.

The most formal business organization is the *corporation*. In many cases, being incorporated can limit your personal liability. Setting up a corporation requires a charter from your state, and you must select a board of directors and officers and issue shares of stock. Filing requirements and conditions vary from state to state.

Contact an attorney to select the best business organization for you.

## Insurance and legal help

Your business organization will determine what insurance you need to protect your personal assets. Review with your attorney what insurance you will need to start your newsletter. Proper insurance can protect you from a lawsuit, and your attorney will help you protect your assets. Review your insurance carefully before you start your newsletter.

## Licensing requirements

Check with the town or city clerk's office to determine what licenses, if any, are required to start a newsletter business. Licensing requirements vary from state to state, from city to city, from town to town. In some states, businesses are required to register the company or owner's name. Your city or town clerk is the best starting place to find out the requirements.

## The copyright certificate

The owner holds the exclusive right, granted by law, to make and dispose of copies of a literary work. By owning the copyright, you can forbid anyone from making copies of your newsletter. This will prevent people from making copies of your newsletter and handing them out to others.

You can prepare the Form SE copyright certificate yourself. The form asks for basic information, such as the name of the newsletter, your name as author, publication date, place of publication, citizenship of author, and your address. Instead of hiring an attorney to apply for you, you can do it yourself. Review the copyright certificate shown in Figure 1-1.

This form is used for periodicals, such as newsletters, which are published at regular intervals of less than 1 year under the same general title. Copyright is not given to the title of your newsletter but to the copyrightable contents of an issue. You can get more information on how to copyright your newsletter by writing to the Copyright Office, Library of Congress, Washington, D.C. 20559. Your newsletter title can be registered as a trademark at the U.S. Patent and Trademark Office, Washington, D.C. 20231.

Print the copyright notice in your newsletter. The best way to ensure that your newsletter is covered by copyright is to have your newsletter bear the copyright notice, such as © John Doe 1999, on the title page, first text page, or the title heading. When you forget to use the copyright notice you lose protection for that issue.

## Taxes

You will be required to file your income tax annually. Hire an accountant to set up your records so that you can file your taxes on time. You only pay taxes on your profit, which is the difference between sales or revenues and expenses. Revenues are the result of subscriptions sold for the year. Expenses are the normal business costs of advertising, postage, printing, office supplies, and the like. Make certain that you include only business expenses for your newsletter business, and not personal expenses such as a gift for your uncle's fiftieth birthday! The key to keeping tax records accurate is to clearly separate business from personal expenses.

Keep your records up to date by recording your revenues and expenses daily, or at the very least, monthly. Too often, newsletter owners delay their accounting week after week, and get too far be-

**FORM SE**

UNITED STATES COPYRIGHT OFFICE

REGISTRATION NUMBER

_____

U

EFFECTIVE DATE OF REGISTRATION

Month          Day          Year

**DO NOT WRITE ABOVE THIS LINE. IF YOU NEED MORE SPACE, USE A SEPARATE CONTINUATION SHEET.**

**1**

**TITLE OF THIS SERIAL ▼**

Volume ▼          Number ▼          Date on Copies ▼          Frequency of Publication ▼

**PREVIOUS OR ALTERNATIVE TITLES ▼**

**2**

**a**

**NAME OF AUTHOR ▼**

**DATES OF BIRTH AND DEATH**
Year Born ▼          Year Died ▼

Was this contribution to the work a "work made for hire"?
☐ Yes
☐ No

**AUTHOR'S NATIONALITY OR DOMICILE**
Name of Country
OR { Citizen of ▶_____
     { Domiciled in ▶_____

**WAS THIS AUTHOR'S CONTRIBUTION TO THE WORK**
Anonymous?      ☐ Yes ☐ No
Pseudonymous?  ☐ Yes ☐ No
If the answer to either of these questions is "Yes," see detailed instructions

**NOTE**

Under the law, the "author" of a work "made for hire" is generally the employer, not the employee (see instructions) For any part of this work that was "made for hire" check "Yes" in the space provided, give the employer (or other person for whom the work was prepared) as "Author" of that part, and leave the space for dates of birth and death blank

**NATURE OF AUTHORSHIP**   Briefly describe nature of the material created by this author in which copyright is claimed. ▼
☐ Collective Work      Other:

**b**

**NAME OF AUTHOR ▼**

**DATES OF BIRTH AND DEATH**
Year Born ▼          Year Died ▼

Was this contribution to the work a "work made for hire"?
☐ Yes
☐ No

**AUTHOR'S NATIONALITY OR DOMICILE**
Name of country
OR { Citizen of ▶_____
     { Domiciled in ▶_____

**WAS THIS AUTHOR'S CONTRIBUTION TO THE WORK**
Anonymous?      ☐ Yes ☐ No
Pseudonymous?  ☐ Yes ☐ No
If the answer to either of these questions is "Yes," see detailed instructions

**NATURE OF AUTHORSHIP**   Briefly describe nature of the material created by this author in which copyright is claimed. ▼
☐ Collective Work      Other:

**c**

**NAME OF AUTHOR ▼**

**DATES OF BIRTH AND DEATH**
Year Born ▼          Year Died ▼

Was this contribution to the work a "work made for hire"?
☐ Yes
☐ No

**AUTHOR'S NATIONALITY OR DOMICILE**
Name of Country
OR { Citizen of ▶_____
     { Domiciled in ▶_____

**WAS THIS AUTHOR'S CONTRIBUTION TO THE WORK**
Anonymous?      ☐ Yes ☐ No
Pseudonymous?  ☐ Yes ☐ No
If the answer to either of these questions is "Yes," see detailed instructions

**NATURE OF AUTHORSHIP**   Briefly describe nature of the material created by this author in which copyright is claimed. ▼
☐ Collective Work      Other:

**3**

**a**

**YEAR IN WHICH CREATION OF THIS ISSUE WAS COMPLETED**   This information must be given in all cases.
◀ Year

**b**

**DATE AND NATION OF FIRST PUBLICATION OF THIS PARTICULAR ISSUE**
Complete this information ONLY if this work has been published.
Month ▶_____ Day ▶_____ Year ▶_____
◀ Nation

**4**

See instructions before completing this space

**COPYRIGHT CLAIMANT(S)** Name and address must be given even if the claimant is the same as the author given in space 2.▼

**TRANSFER** If the claimant(s) named here in space 4 are different from the author(s) named in space 2, give a brief statement of how the claimant(s) obtained ownership of the copyright.▼

APPLICATION RECEIVED

ONE DEPOSIT RECEIVED

TWO DEPOSITS RECEIVED

REMITTANCE NUMBER AND DATE

*DO NOT WRITE HERE OFFICE USE ONLY*

**MORE ON BACK ▶**   • Complete all applicable spaces (numbers 5-11) on the reverse side of this page
• See detailed instructions          • Sign the form at line 10

DO NOT WRITE HERE

Page 1 of_____pages

*Fig. 1-1. Copyright form SE.*

EXAMINED BY

CHECKED BY

☐ CORRESPONDENCE
   Yes

FORM SE

FOR
COPYRIGHT
OFFICE
USE
ONLY

**DO NOT WRITE ABOVE THIS LINE. IF YOU NEED MORE SPACE, USE A SEPARATE CONTINUATION SHEET.**

**PREVIOUS REGISTRATION**   Has registration for this issue, or for an earlier version of this particular issue, already been made in the Copyright Office?

☐ **Yes** ☐ **No**  If your answer is "Yes," why is another registration being sought? (Check appropriate box) ▼

**a.** ☐ This is the first published version of an issue previously registered in unpublished form.

**b.** ☐ This is the first application submitted by this author as copyright claimant.

**c.** ☐ This is a changed version of this issue, as shown by space 6 on this application.

If your answer is "Yes," give: **Previous Registration Number** ▼          **Year of Registration** ▼

**5**

**DERIVATIVE WORK OR COMPILATION**   Complete both space 6a & 6b for a derivative work; complete only 6b for a compilation.

**a.**  **Preexisting Material**   Identify any preexisting work or works that this work is based on or incorporates. ▼

**b.**  **Material Added to This Work**   Give a brief, general statement of the material that has been added to this work and in which copyright is claimed. ▼

See instructions
before completing
this space

**6**

## —space deleted—

**7**

**REPRODUCTION FOR USE OF BLIND OR PHYSICALLY HANDICAPPED INDIVIDUALS**       A signature on this form at space 10, and a check in one of the boxes here in space 8, constitutes a non-exclusive grant of permission to the Library of Congress to reproduce and distribute solely for the blind and physically handicapped and under the conditions and limitations prescribed by the regulations of the Copyright Office: (1) copies of the work identified in space 1 of this application in Braille (or similar tactile symbols); or (2) phonorecords embodying a fixation of a reading of that work; or (3) both.

a ☐ Copies and Phonorecords          b ☐ Copies Only          c ☐ Phonorecords Only

See instructions

**8**

**DEPOSIT ACCOUNT**   If the registration fee is to be charged to a Deposit Account established in the Copyright Office, give name and number of Account.
**Name** ▼                                         **Account Number** ▼

**9**

**CORRESPONDENCE**   Give name and address to which correspondence about this application should be sent.   Name Address Apt City State Zip ▼

Area Code & Telephone Number ▶

Be sure to
give your
daytime phone
◀ number

**CERTIFICATION\***  I, the undersigned, hereby certify that I am the

Check one ▶

☐ author
☐ other copyright claimant
☐ owner of exclusive right(s)
☐ authorized agent of

of the work identified in this application and that the statements made by me in this application are correct to the best of my knowledge.

Name of author or other copyright claimant, or owner of exclusive right(s) ▲

**10**

**Typed or printed name and date** ▼ If this application gives a date of publication in space 3, do not sign and submit it before that date.

date ▶

Handwritten signature (X) ▼

**MAIL
CERTIFI-
CATE TO**

Name ▼

Number Street Apartment Number ▼

City State ZIP ▼

**Certificate
will be
mailed in
window
envelope**

**YOU MUST:**
• Complete all necessary spaces
• Sign your application in space 10
**SEND ALL 3 ELEMENTS
IN THE SAME PACKAGE:**
1. Application form
2. Non-refundable $10 filing fee
   in check or money order
   payable to Register of Copyrights
3. Deposit material
**MAIL TO:**
Register of Copyrights
Library of Congress
Washington, D.C. 20559

**11**

\* 17 U.S.C. § 506(e)  Any person who knowingly makes a false representation of a material fact in the application for copyright registration provided for by section 409, or in any written statement filed in connection with the application, shall be fined not more than $2,500.

July 1989—75,000                                                                                                ☆U.S. GOVERNMENT PRINTING OFFICE: 1989—241-428 00001

*Fig. 1-1. (Continued)*

hind to catch up. You need this information to make decisions. Try to reconcile your bank statement as soon as you receive it.

## Keep a separate checking account for your business

Open a checking account for your business; some newsletter owners name the account after the title of their newsletter, for example, *The Consultant Newsletter* account. Do not pay personal bills from this account. Pay your monthly dry cleaning bill from your personal bank account. On the other hand, pay for printing your first newsletter from the *The Consultant Newsletter* account because it is clearly a business expense. When you pay expenses, get a bill or a receipt. As a general rule, keep your personal finances separate from your business finances.

## Help from the government

State and federal funds support various publications, consulting services, and educational opportunities. Many of these are free or offered at a very small charge. For example, an organization called SCORE (Service Corps of Retired Executives) can provide free counseling for your business from a retired executive with experience in printing and publishing. SCORE offers seminars and workshops to help new business ventures to get started successfully. Call the U.S. Small Business Administration in your area to ask about the services available from and the location of the SCORE office nearest to you. Retired people have a great deal to offer, and you can take advantage of their knowledge and skills.

The federal government also offers reports, pamphlets, and articles on small businesses and home-based businesses at nominal charges, and some are even free. For a listing of these excellent publications, write to Superintendent of Documents, U.S. Government Printing Office, Washington, D.C. 20402. More information on government information and services may be found at the reference desk of your local or regional library.

Your state government may also offer help in the form of seminars, information, and even business and college courses. Call or write the small business or commerce department of your state government for information. Use the services, knowledge, tools, and resources of local, state, and federal governments.

## Look for a need

The successful newsletter fulfills important needs in the marketplace. I received a newsletter, recently, from a home-based newsletter owner, that dealt, in a general sense, with the problems associated with owning a small business. There is no question that millions of small businesses need help to compete successfully in a competitive marketplace, but they are hesitant to subscribe to a newsletter that fails to meet *specific* needs. A general discussion of problems in itself is fine, but a newsletter must also help subscribers with particulars. The small business newsletter might deal with cutting costs, improving quality of the product, motivating and rewarding employees, and developing goals.

It is not enough simply to choose a newsletter subject you feel comfortable about. You must also have enough information to serve the subscribers, and a clear *concept strategy*. We will discuss this further in Chapter 2, but the closer you stick to a strong, well-developed initial concept, the more successful your newsletter will be. For example, a Kentucky financial planner has developed a newsletter with the concept of offering investment information for those in the middle-income bracket. Each issue offers the latest information on various investment opportunities appropriate for this bracket from stocks and bonds, to IRAs, mutual funds, and the like. The newsletter is only one year old but it is growing steadily.

## Compete with yourself not with others

I have found in my seminars on newsletters that some students spend too much time comparing their ideas or newsletters with those of others. Don't fall into this trap. Focus instead on competing with yourself to do a little better each day. When you get an idea for your newsletter, make it even better by defining the content you plan to use. Focus on the reasons people would subscribe to *your* newsletter rather than another publication. Focus on your newsletter *features,* such as stock information and return on investment—these are reasons subscribers will choose *your* newsletter. Get to know the benefits to your reader; knowledge of these benefits will help you succeed. A list of benefits for a newsletter on selling that is geared toward sales professionals follows.

1. Techniques of psychological selling
2. The keys to successful communication
3. How to handle objections successfully
4. How to get new customers
5. The secrets of powerful negotiation
6. How to read the customer's thought patterns
7. Gathering knowledge to earn more money
8. How to sell services as well as products
9. How to make money and buy the things you want
10. How to give a dynamic and profitable presentation

Looking closely at the various benefits gives you an opportunity to discover the important content areas for your newsletter. The list above shows the reader how this publication can help him or her to become a better sales professional, and earn more money and status. Successful newsletters present important benefits such as these issue after issue.

## Review your feelings right now

Perhaps you are not ready to start a newsletter immediately, but would like to get warmed up a bit before taking on the full task. Why not start a family newsletter, a newsletter wherein you would write about news in your family, for example, new promotions, births, vacations, and family projects. Or you might volunteer to do a newsletter for your church, or local service club or association. The experience you get from writing articles will help you prepare for your own newsletter in the future. You can do it!

## Summary

The newsletter business can be exciting and profitable. Think about the best possible subject for you. There is very little equipment needed for success. You sell information, and you must keep your readers satisfied with your product. Remember to get the required insurance, licenses, and permits. Home-based newsletter businesses can grow into large publishing enterprises. Many small newsletters survive and grow. A successful newsletter can be yours!

# 2

# Choosing a newsletter subject and targeting your market

The newsletter is a vehicle to help you reach a group of readers in a special way. This group, the target market, looks forward to your publication each week, month, or quarter, to learn more about your subject or field. For example, a woman from New York recently started a newsletter for adjunct faculty, teachers of college-level courses in various subjects from English and history to accounting. Since these instructors are trained in their specialty, not necessarily in education, they enjoy and benefit from ideas to help them teach better. One recent issue featured handling the first class; another showed how to structure time to teach a difficult history or English class. The newsletter owner found a need among teachers and filled it.

This chapter will give you many ideas to develop a newsletter topic, and some insights into the newsletter market, the people who will spend their hard-earned money to subscribe.

## Why use a newsletter format to reach your audience?

A newsletter is a specialized written report that is prepared for a specific group or organization. A newsletter is special because it presents difficult-to-find information; it may include forecasts, predictions, analysis, and research. A newsletter is well planned and directs the important information to the subscribers. To survive, a newsletter must continue to offer insights and exciting material that is unavailable in other public publishing outlets such as magazines, journals, and newspapers.

## How does a newsletter differ from a newspaper?

A newspaper is usually issued daily or weekly on newsprint and contains news of a community or field, with comments, features, and photographs. It often includes advertising. Advertising, a paid form of nonpersonal presentation of goods and services by an identified sponsor, is an important source of income for the newspaper. A local newsletter, on the other hand, if it runs advertisements at all, might include some items from the local food market, car agency, hardware store, pizza parlor, or fast-food restaurant. Most newsletters, however, do not include advertising.

A newsletter can be written and prepared by one person, while a newspaper is usually written by a number of writers and prepared by a specialized staff, from printers to artists. A newsletter can be owned by one person; a newspaper is usually owned by a number of people. A newsletter is written for a specialized audience, for example, coin collectors, investors, or bankers, while most newspapers are written for a general audience, for example, all the people living within a town or city.

## When did the first newsletter start?

The first newsletter, *The Boston News-Letter,* was published in American colonial times, from 1704–1774. The first business newsletter was the *South Carolina Current*, started on July 30, 1774. The popular *Kiplinger Newsletter*, started in 1923, has become a role model for other newsletters because of its long life, excellent content, and fine reputation.

## Read other newsletters

The best way to find out about newsletters is to read as many as possible. Some newsletters are available at your local, regional, or city library. Ask your reference librarian for a listing of available newsletters. The reference librarian may not permit newsletters to circulate, but will permit you to read them at the library. You cannot copy the newsletter since most newsletters are copyrighted.

## Sharing information is essential

As a newsletter owner you are sharing information with your readers or subscribers. You must know enough about your subject so that you share *new*, relevant information that is not available in other media, such as magazines, radio, videos, or television.

Watch your tone while sharing your information. Don't preach to your subscribers. Use a tone that shows respect for your readers' opinions. For example, a Connecticut newsletter owner, Janet N., started a newsletter for supervisors that shares timely information to help them become successful. Recent issues have explored such topics as supervisors' loyalty; supervisors and the law; supervisors' common mistakes in the 1990s; handling change; hiring and keeping the best people; rating yourself as boss; cutting costs; getting quality work from yourself and others; training employees to compete globally; and keeping workers thinking safety while working productively. In order to keep her supervision-oriented newsletter successful, Janet regularly tests the readability of each monthly issue by calling a sample of readers to get their evaluation of her latest work. Keep working hard to maintain a rapport with your subscribers.

## What are the various types of newsletters?

There are two basic groups, the for-profit and the not-for-profit. Once you decide to publish a for-profit newsletter, it will need subscriptions. Consider the following subscription-type newsletters:

1. The *investment* newsletter gives advice on purchasing stocks, bonds, or mutual funds.
2. The *business* newsletter gives information on managing businesses (see Figure 2-1).
3. The *consumer* newsletter advises the general consumer (see Figure 2-2).
4. The *affinity* or *hobby* newsletter gives information to readers who enjoy a particular hobby (see Figure 2-3).
5. The *instructional* newsletter gives information, for example, on building a log cabin or becoming a supervisor.

Not-for-profit newsletters, which offer valuable information to readers who are not subscribers, are very important in newsletter publishing. These newsletters can be a valuable tool for selling products and services. Consider the following:

1. The *organization* newsletter is published by hospitals, schools, and nursing homes to keep the public abreast of the latest news and developments in their fields (see Figure 2-4).
2. Another type is the *franchise* newsletter, where a franchise owner publishes information for other franchise owners or for retailers (see Figure 2-5).
3. Finally, there's the *public relations* newsletter that is published for current, past, and potential customers (see Figure 2-6).

Let's summarize these types of newsletters:

| *For-profit newsletter* | *Not-for-profit newsletter* |
| --- | --- |
| Investment/financial | Public relations |
| Business | Franchise |
| Consumer | Organizational |
| Affinity/hobby | |
| Instructional | |

Keep in mind that a subscription newsletter must be marketed aggressively and have the right content, so that your customers will be willing to part with their hard-earned money. Many newsletter own-

# IT'S YOUR BUSINESS™

Vol. 1  No. 1                          **NEWSLETTER**                          Aug/Sept 1990

Informing, inspiring, and encouraging people pursuing their own business by providing opportunities to learn from the real experiences of people who are doing it.

CONTENTS:                                    page

- - - - - - - - - - - - - - -

**HE BID $100,000 AND GOT THE JOB, ONLY HE HAD NEVER DONE A JOB OVER $10,000 BEFORE**

It's true, a friend of my husband, named Mark, has a landscape maintenance business several hundred miles from where we live, and he also does small landscape installation jobs on the side. He knew he had things to learn before he tackled a large job, but the opportunity to bid a large commercial job came up and he wanted to bid it.

He needed help bidding such a large job, so who was he going to go to for help? He couldn't go to another competing landscaper and ask for advice of course. So he called up my husband, John, who also happens to do landscape work. John, however, has done some large jobs and was able to give Mark tips on how to bid it right.

Mark bid it, and got the job. Then he needed advice again on installing the irrigation system. John was happy to help him out and even flew up to consult with Mark for a couple of days. Mark was able to complete the job successfully, making money in the process.

Having another experienced person give advice and suggestions really helped Mark out.

And it has worked both ways. Mark has given John tips on how to improve the efficiency of John's own landscape maintenance business as well. They have been able to help each other because they each have had their own unique experiences and learned important lessons.

Being able to get advice and ideas for improving one's business from another business person like that is a valuable form of support.

Even business people having different types of businesses can provide each other with valuable, useful information. Another person's techniques can be modified to apply to your own business, or can also spark new ideas for you.

For instance, you might notice some innovative yet inexpensive way someone is packaging and displaying their product for sale, which you could implement for a product of your own. Or you may learn of another person's methods of gaining more customers through some unusual advertising technique which you could duplicate.

And it helps to learn from **reality** - real tangible experiences, not just theories.

A study done by Harvard Business School showed that people learn much more from people who give testimonials about their

*Fig. 2-1. A business newsletter.*

own experiences than the traditional methods of learning through text-books and lectures which speak of theory more than reality.

But you may not personally know a lot of business people with whom you can trade ideas or advice. So how do you find these people so you can interact with them? There may be people out there with some good ideas which could help you but how do you plug into this kind of information? Where would you look?

You could search through the newspaper for articles on people in business . . .

That can sometimes be helpful. I do that myself. I love to find such information as it often motivates me and gives me ideas to try on our own two businesses that John and I run.

But I find it isn't enough. I want more. I really enjoy getting information on positive things and good ideas people have come up with, especially in relation to a business they have started. And I don't think I am alone in this enjoyment either. I would guess that a lot of people, like you who are reading this now, can find such information about people in business interesting and valuable as there is plenty that can be learned from other people's stories that can make one's own situation better, which is what most of us want.

What a great way to learn -- from experience, and to learn from the experience of others can only compound that advantage.

So I came up with an idea which embodies these concepts. It is simple. My idea is to publish a newsletter which focuses on real people, and their experience in business!

But there's more. This is no ordinary newsletter written by 1 or 2 people. That could limit the content of the newsletter somewhat.

The content of "It's Your Business", however, will be potentially unlimited,

as it will come from a growing network of many, many different people in business because the letters or articles making up the newsletter will be written primarily by the subscribers to the newsletter. What better way to find out what motivated, forward-moving people in business are doing and how they are doing it than to read articles written by people in business that tell you!

By reading this newsletter, you will be given the opportunity to improve your own business situation by learning about what has worked and what hasn't worked for other people. The lines of communication can really start to open up, and lead to specific sections on questions and answers, making contact with one another, and more. Maybe you have your own ideas on special sections we could put into the newsletter. I'd like to hear what you would like to have. This is a user-friendly publication!

As you know by now, this newsletter focuses on a subject I love, and I think it is a dynamite one, and now I need feedback FROM YOU to really propel this thing into a super information-packed newsletter.

Each of you has something unique to offer, some information about yourself and your business which is interesting and worthwhile. That is what I want to hear about from you. Don't think that you have to write an article, however, it is certainly not a requirement in order to subscribe! But if you have something important you would like to write about, please do!

I envision my subscribers as being people who live all over the country, many of whom will be sending me their writings about their experiences, successes, and failures so that I may compile them into the newsletter and help generate a positive, interesting, helpful, exciting, inspiring tool to put into your hands.

Imagine drawing from the experiences of so many people!

And I want you to know that the articles I get from you do not have to be written as though you are writing a report or

*Fig. 2-1. (Continued)*

# THE KIPLINGER WASHINGTON LETTER

*Circulated weekly to business clients since 1923—Vol. 68, No. 4*

THE KIPLINGER WASHINGTON EDITORS
1729 H St., N.W., Washington, D.C. 20006-3938 Tel: 202-887-6400

Dear Client:                                          Washington, Jan. 25, 1991

    <u>Highpoints this Letter</u>:  An unofficial expansion of war goals.
Probably no tax increase to pay for war.  $15 oil following the conflict.
Help for banks temporarily short of cash.  New rules for shaky loans.
Lower interest rates ahead.  And further progress against trade deficits.

    <u>Chasing Iraq out of Kuwait is not our ONLY objective</u> in the war,
though it's the only stated goal, along with restoring the Kuwaiti gov't.
    <u>The other objective will remain unofficial</u> but is JUST as real:
<u>Getting rid of Saddam</u>...whatever it takes to boot him out.
Fact is, he no longer has a choice of leaving Kuwait and keeping his job.
Despite official denials by military leaders and others in our own gov't,
overthrowing Saddam is now a goal agreed to by everyone in the coalition.
That includes the Saudis, Egyptians and other Arabs...Saddam HAS to go.
    <u>Top officials count on freeing Kuwait by spring</u>, after rooting out
Iraqi ground forces, tanks and artillery capable of firing poison gas.
Insiders on war plans & strategy will remain guarded in public comments.
    <u>In private talks, they figure we'll soon have Iraq on the run</u>.

    <u>Oil prices will probably bounce around in the $20s</u> for a while.
Ample supplies and release of gov't stocks will prevent big price spikes,
but concern over possible disruptions will keep major traders on edge.
And refineries will keep some extra oil in their stocks "just in case."
    <u>After the war, oil will drop to $15 per barrel</u> or even lower.
Won't stay there for long...but long enough to help cool off inflation.
There will be plenty of oil around, and demand slacks off in the spring.

    <u>Look at who's doing what to aid the war effort</u>:
<u>Altogether, 685,000 armed personnel</u>.  Over 475,000 from the U.S.
Britain is next...35,000.  Then Egypt, 30,000.  Saudi Arabia and Syria,
20,000 each.  France 15,000.  Turkey has huge forces massed on its border
with Iraq.  Also small numbers of troops from Bangladesh and elsewhere.
    <u>Plus planes & ships</u>.  Most from U.S.  Britain plays a major role.
Also Saudis, Kuwaitis, Egyptians, French, Canadians, Italians and others.
    <u>And money</u>.  Nearly $30 billion is pledged in cash or supplies,
including help for front-line nations, such as Egypt, Turkey and Jordan.
Most of it comes from Saudi Arabia and Kuwait, then Japan and Germany.
    <u>No one knows the cost</u>.  Estimates run from $20 to $90 billion,
depending on how long war lasts and how much equipment will be replaced.

    <u>A war tax is not likely</u>, though there's a lot of talk about it.
The President is against a tax hike, and Congress won't force the issue.
    <u>Interest rates will decline further</u>, assuming a fairly short war.
The recession and lower inflation this year will help push rates lower.
    <u>Federal Reserve will ease up on credit</u> slowly and cautiously.
    <u>The dollar will probably strengthen</u> as the war intensifies...
safe haven for investors around the world whenever there's an emergency.

*Fig. 2-2. A consumer newsletter.*

<u>Look for a trade deficit of roughly $85 billion this year</u>...
down from about $100 billion last year and $110 billion the year before.
Cheaper oil helps.  And our merchandise deficit with Japan will shrink
as Japanese auto and other manufacturers increase production in the U.S.
<u>Next year, down to $60 billion</u> as exports move ahead strongly.
Progress on the trade deficit is one reason the economy will brighten.
<u>Note that oil will remain the wild card</u> in the trade figures.
The '90 trade deficit would be $50 billion lower if oil were taken out.

<u>War won't force up shipping rates</u> or disrupt movement of freight
by rail, ship or plane.  There'll be exceptions, of course, but very few.
<u>After the war, a reassessment of U.S. sealift capacity</u>...vessels
and personnel for hauling vast amounts of materials during an emergency.
<u>Also reevaluation of our reserve fleet</u> because of disappointment
with the age and usefulness of vessels.  Fleet size, the mix of ships,
extent of maintenance and readiness will all come up for close scrutiny.
<u>Merchant marine may be beefed up</u> by the Dep't of Transportation
and Congress.  Seafarers may get some benefits reservists now receive,
including assurances of getting their civilian jobs back after the war.

<u>Retail business will probably remain sluggish until midyear</u>...
heavy debt burdens and job worries will keep consumers on the sidelines.
That's why stores are slashing inventories and discounting so heavily.
Discounters will do better than others...appealing to bargain hunters.
<u>Quite a few stores are on thin ice</u>...more bankruptcies ahead.
<u>A boom for close-out specialists</u> who pick the carcass clean.

<u>A glut of unsold new cars</u> on dealers' lots and showrooms.
<u>Models in greatest surplus</u> are Chrysler LeBaron and New Yorker.
Dodge Shadow and Daytona.  Plymouth Laser.  All Eagles.  Ford Mustang
and Probe.  Mercury Grand Marquis.  Chevrolet Camaro, Corsica, Beretta
and Caprice.  Geo Storm.  Buick LeSabre and Riviera.  Cadillac Allante.
Pontiac Firebird.  Also Mitsubishis, Subarus, Isuzus, Suzukis and Audis.
<u>This is a guide</u> to cars that dealers are most anxious to sell.
In many cases, automakers are dishing out bonuses to work down surpluses.

<u>Rules on access for the disabled to new or remodeled buildings</u>...
grocery stores, hotels, restaurants & bars, office buildings, theaters.
Proposal of the Architectural & Transportation Barriers Compliance Board
was published in Jan. 22 Federal Register...available at main libraries.
<u>Most of the proposal will stick</u>...new buildings and renovations.
<u>For stores</u>...wheelchair-width checkout lanes in supermarkets.
<u>Hotels, restaurants</u>...5% of rooms and tables must be accessible.
<u>Taverns</u>...some low tables or bars for drinkers in wheelchairs.
<u>Office buildings</u>...bathrooms must be accessible to the disabled.
If six or more public phones, at least one must be equipped for the deaf.
<u>Public hearings will be held around the country</u> Feb. 11-March 7.
If you want to find out about the places and times, phone 800-USA-ABLE.

<u>Rules with even more impact on business will be proposed in Feb.</u>
<u>Details on how employers must adjust for disabled employees</u>...
physical or mental.  The Equal Employment Opportunity Comm. will require
that best-qualified job applicants be hired, regardless of disabilities.
<u>EEOC is braced for a fight</u> with employer lobbies and others.
It will argue that the '90 law doesn't allow any room for backing down.

*Fig. 2-2. (Continued)*

# GINNY

## Doll Collectors Club

# NEWSLETTER

| Ann Smith      Editor & Publisher | 21 Main St.   Dover, NH 03820 |

Issue 8    August 1991

## SUMMERTIME NEWS FROM GINNY

Ginny is getting very excited about the Festival. She hopes lots of her friends will be coming. Aware that many of the Ginny Mommies live far away, she hopes they are working on contest ideas, at least. If you are new to our club, or just didn't get to read the last newsletter, look later in this issue for contest rules and Festival information.

Seldom a week goes by that Ginny and I don't hear from some club member, or potential member, by mail or phone. It makes being a Ginny lover so much more fun when the enthusiasm is shared. That is why I am going to give a lot of membership news this time. Then, hopefully, even more of you will write to me and share news and information for us all.

## TABLE OF CONTENTS

Please give special attention to the ads this month. There are many great new Ginny clothes being designed. If they sound nice to you and you don't sew, write the designer and see if she will make you an outfit. If not, contact me and I will either make it for you or find someone who will.

This is the time of year for doll shows, auctions, sales, exhibits and fairs. Please send me news of your "great finds" or near misses, or the prizes you've won. We all love news of this sort.

16" GINNY
A Little Swiss
one-piece dress

PATTERN
easy to make

#35....... $1.75
postpaid
Catalog
$1.25

Peggy Jones
20 Wilson Rd.
Rochester, NY
14610

*Fig. 2-3. An affinity, or hobby, newsletter.*

# The Haverhill Rehab Hospital
# *Health Newsletter*

**Publication for our employees, clients, and associates**

Gregory P. Bond, Editor, 1 Water Street, Haverhill, MA 1830          508-372-7957

# Minding you own time

All of us have the same amount of time each day, only 24 hours. The ability to use your time correctly may spell the difference between success and failure on your job. Time will wait for you if you earn it. Successful people consider time a very precious commodity--a commodity that is utilized to its ultimate degree. Some executives plan the things they want to accomplish during a normal work day. They put a priority on their tasks, finishing the first priority before going on to the second and third. Once a system like this is in operation it becomes a work style that enhances use of your time.

Some executives can do more than one thing at a time. You can add up a column of figures while waiting for someone to come to the phone. Another trick is to wait until you have sufficient material before hand-delivering paperwork. It is not how much work you do; it is how "smart" you work.

Be observant of the people around you. Ask yourself how other workers would handle a particular job. Each person you meet has unique talents, and may have some tricks or secrets that might help you save time.

Try time periods of uninterrupted work. Some executives find that they can use time wisely in uninterrupted 60 to 90 minute periods. Close the door for either 60 or 90 minutes. Permit no interruptions at all. Let your secretary handle your telephone calls and visitors. After your uninterrupted work period, allow 15 or 20 minutes for handling notes from your secretary about phone calls, visitors, and so forth. Once you handle these minor details, you can start your next work period. This formula will take discipline, but the results you will achieve by having

uninterrupted work periods will pay large dividends.

Many executives feel that long hours of work may be avoided if time can be used effectively. Too much time can be wasted on tasks that are unimportant or can be done at another time. If certain jobs are set up in the morning and they are important, don't be sidetracked. Make certain that you stay on the right path to accomplish the jobs that have the highest priority.

It is common for people to get involved in work that they like and do well. Avoid neglecting work that is difficult or time-consuming. You may need the added exposure of this work to round out your experience.

Think of time as money. Have you ever seen people destroy money? People destroy money by wasting valuable time or doing an easy job the hard way and taking twice as long to complete it. If people were fired for their carelessness of work or foolish wasting of time, the situation would rapidly correct itself.

An executive is too highly paid to do small jobs. Learn to delegate work that can be done by someone else so that you can take advantage of your knowledge and skills in important areas.

A young business executive claims that he is always trying to save time by addressing himself to new ways of doing things. He is continually trying to find faster, easier, more efficient ways of doing things. Some executives are content to handle routine jobs the way they were handled in the past. Too many times, routine jobs are handled in the same manner for years without any investigation about new ways to do the job. Why duplicate efforts? Why not do it the best way?

*Fig. 2-4. An organization newsletter.*

Find out how you are spending your day. Is too much time being spent on routine jobs, filing, answering the phone, answering simple questions, and the like? Once you find out what is taking most of your time, ask yourself how you can better use your valuable time. A successful executive must know how to control time.

Many executives spend valuable time doing jobs that are not required or are a waste of valuable time. An executive must determine whether the job is necessary, and if it is not, should discontinue it. Some executives find better ways to do certain jobs by trying new methods of handling the work. Think things through until you come up with an answer that is not commonplace. Come up with new ideas that will help you do your job better.

Never get bogged down by the pessimist who will shoot holes in every idea, plan, project, or assignment within the company. The pessimist wastes the time of those foolish enough to listen. The pessimist will spread gloom over any subject. Try to develop your assignments based on the activities and results you want to achieve.

Do not slow yourself down by doing jobs that should be done by someone else. Demand that others perform their work even though you may have to wait for their work to perform your job. Never give the impression that you will pick up the slack and do others' work. Demand that others perform their own duties.

Try to do two or three things at once to save time. A left-handed person can run a business machine with his right hand while writing information with his left. Organize your desk so that you have easy access to your equipment.

Time can be saved by putting together all the necessary information before you visit or telephone a person. Don't ask someone an important question on the fly; wait until you can discuss it in private. People react differently when approached with other people around than alone in their offices. Be ready for the meeting or the phone conversation to avoid a second or third phone call.

Proper communications saves time. When you communicate to someone, consider the background of the person to whom you are speaking. Speak slowly, clearly and simply to be certain of being understood. Talk of pictures and illustrations to artists. Speak of themes and ideas when talking to writers. You will know when you are talking someone's language by the nod of a head or the answer to your question. Know that to communicate effectively, you must talk the person's language.

Summary of ways to control your time. Proper planning of things to do and listing priorities of jobs save time. Become conscious of time, attempt to use every minute. Do several jobs at the same time. Think of time as money, and try to work for a solid block of time without interruption. Try to beat your own records: Save additional time each day, and look for faster ways of doing your jobs.

Tricks of saving time may be as simple as (1) buying a good watch, (2) cutting down on personal chatter and beginning work on time, (3) making use of the reference librarian, (4) asking questions, (5) making use of good ideas, (6) using your commuting time and lunch periods, (7) changing your normal work schedule, (8) seeing a job through to completion, (9) concentrating on one task at a time, (10) developing a good rapport with others, (11) making use of your telephone for quick answers and appointments, (12) using good memory joggers, (13) knowing the right people to talk to when you need information, (14) delegating tasks that can be handled more efficiently and speedily by others, (15) trying new ways of doing tasks, (16) avoiding the office pessimist, (17) avoiding becoming so efficient that you take on jobs that are assigned to others, (18) being prepared before you telephone a person or sit down at a meeting, and (19) communicating based on a person's understanding and background, in short, talking the person's language.

It is very easy to waste valuable time. It is much more difficult to become time-conscious--to work toward a full day of work with a minimum amount of wasted time. When you work for another you are in business for yourself, and you are selling your services for a set salary per week. It is up to you not to waste any of your precious time and money.

*Fig. 2-4. (Continued)*

# Designer Store Newsletter

**NOVEMBER 1989 - WINTER QUARTER**                    ©Copyright 1989 Harley-Davidson, Inc.

# YOUR BUSINESS

*By Bob Michel*

## 'TWAS THE NIGHT BEFORE MOTORCLOTHES™'

'Twas the month before Christmas and all through the land, Harley dealers were anxious for MotorClothes in hand. The stores had been decorated for the season with care, in hopes that holiday shoppers soon would be there. Lots of work has been done, but you can't settle back. Plenty more to do filling holiday sacks. You ordered your Motorclothes in August this year, and you're ready to move them when they get here. But what to my wondering eyes do I see? Not all of you are ready, how can this be! Find your new product spec sheets and study them well. Know your product thoroughly and it's sure to sell. Don't just scratch your head your store must look great. Get ideas at the mall, there's no time to wait! Your merchandise is coming, display it with pride. Make it convenient for customers, those who do or don't ride! Move it all, move it fast, sell it all out! Because turning your inventory is what it's about. And all that was heard as he rode into the night was do what I've said, and everything will be all right!
On Calgary, on Alaskan, on Cafe, on Legend!
*Happy Holidays to all, and to all a profitable night.*

*Fig. 2-5. A franchise newsletter.*

# Harley-Davidson..*Fashion Statement*

### BY JOHN WYCKOFF

*Harley-Davidson was born as a motorcycle. It became a life style and has now evolved, in the eyes of trend setters, into a "fashion statement."*

When all Harley-Davidson stood for was a motorcycle, selling was easy. Buyer and seller spoke the same language and understood each other. As it evolved into a life-style, selling became a bit more complicated but at the same time more rewarding. Now that the name also encompasses a fashion statement, the buyer and seller may find themselves worlds apart.

To be successful in selling Harley-Davidson as fashion you must consider some dynamic changes. Some dealers will not be up to the task; others will find the thought of selling fashion apparel repulsive. However, those who recognize the opportunities to broaden their customer base will profit if they agree to make the appropriate changes in their attitude, display and approach.

Up-scale "yuppie" type buyers respond to things like ads in Playboy, Rolling Stone and Cosmopolitan magazines. Many, if not most, have never seen the inside of a Harley-Davidson store. Their attitudes towards motorcycles are colored by the perception that motorcyclists are stereotypes. We're either "bikers" with all the negative that that implies or "canyon racer" with all the negative that implies.

How do you sell them without selling out yourself? By making some small adjustments in appearances and approach.

First, keep in mind that the up-scale buyer has malls stores as his/her frame of reference. They feel uncomfortable in surroundings that fail to measure up. No, you don't have to be so slick that you look like a Mercedes Benz dealer. You do, however, have to operate a clean, well-arranged and well-lighted store. Your salespeople don't have to wear suits and ties. They do, however, have to set aside the black "t" shirts, jeans and tennis shoes, and instead opt for neat sport shirts (with name tags), casual slacks and shoes.

The second consideration involves the display of the fashion goods. Peg-boards are out; they appear too busy and distracting. Grid systems, while better than peg-board, are less attractive than slat wall for displaying garments. The fashions garments must be displayed full front out. Never attempt to display high-ticket fashions on pipe racks that only show sleeves. The garments that have unusually interesting back should be displayed with back showing and be well lite.

Mirrors are a must. Three mirrors, arranged in a "U" shape. are best. Why? They allow the customer to see him/herself from the sides and back. The Harley-Davidson fashion garments were designed to give the customer a positive self image from all angles. If you don't have the room for the "U" shape, consider building a tall triangle of mirrors and placing them in front of but not parallel to. a wall mirror. This arrangement will create a better image than a simple wall mirror.

Women can be better at selling fashion than men. If there's a woman on your staff encourage her to become involved in the arrangement of the fashion department and perhaps in the sale of fashions as well. The up-scale buyer who is less than comfortable in motorcycle store will feel more at ease when dealing with a woman salesperson.

Service must be lightning fast. When the new customer enters your store he/she must be greeted immediately. Not aggressively; quickly. Their presence must be acknowledged. After that they may wish to browse on their own, without interference, but they must never be ignored.

The last point, although one of the most important, is product knowledge. Up-scale buyers want to know the features and benefits of what they're buying. Partly because it justifies the price and partly because they feel they can make their buying decision if they believe the quality meets their standards. Make certain that each salesperson has a complete understanding of the advantages, benefits and features of the new Motor Clothes.

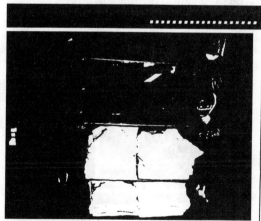

**Where ever possible, fold sweaters and shelve to help them maintain sweater's shape. Also have a hanging DISPLAY of the sweater nearby. (have it hung on a quality hanger.)**

*Fig. 2-5. (Continued)*

December 1994 ─────────────────────────

# Workskills

**Tips from Boardman Temporary Help Services for Managing Your Work**

## *Management of Your Interruptions at Work*

*S*uccessful people have a common skill which sets them apart from their competition: Full concentration on getting the most important things done for today, without excessive concern about the future or the past. This article will give you some ideas about how you can direct your full concentration toward the most important resource you have in your arsenal: your time.

### Set up the priorities for the day
What do you want to accomplish today? What is the most important thing you can do today?

Alice is a sales representative for a large insurance company. She promised her boss to increase insurance policy sales to engineering and technical employees at the local manufacturing company in her city. Alice will spend the full day trying to get appointments with this special group. This will become her number 1 priority.

Fred is an accounts receivable clerk with a large computer company. His important priority is to work on a large account which is more than 60 days overdue on its invoices. Successful people examine their jobs, determine what important priorities are needed, and work on them daily.

### Deal with your interruptions
Just because you choose your priority carefully and begin it first thing in the morning does not mean yesterday's

DIG A WELL
BEFORE
YOU'RE THIRSTY.
*CHINESE PROVERB*

*Fig. 2-6. A public relations newsletter.*

and tomorrow's priorities will not get in the way of your progress.

The phone rings, Sadie in Shipping and Receiving has a question or two on yesterday's receiving reports. Janet in Accounting wants your future projections on the sales in your department. The rabbi's assistant calls, he wants to know whether you plan to attend the banquet at the temple next month. Deal with these minor interruptions, but go back to the number 1 priority you set for yourself at the beginning of the day. In cases where you cannot deal with the interruption quickly, inform the caller there is an urgent project right now, and you will get back to him or her later. Keep going back to your number 1 priority.

### The stacked desk interruption

Fred started his number 1 priority, but after working on it for 30 minutes, he started to look into the pile of papers on his desk. Some of the papers were interesting, one thing lead to another, and his number 1 priority was left unattended. Now, Fred is falling behind in his work.

Take the time to thin out the stack of extra paper on your desk, file the papers you will need in the future, and throw out unnecessary papers, or those for which you can get a duplicate from another source. Stay ahead of your cleaning to avoid the stacked desk interruption.

*Fig. 2-6. (Continued)*

### The too-much-work interruption

The statements so common in numerous offices in the 1990s working world are: "I'm tired. I know I'm doing too much work myself." Little wonder you cannot finish organizing the day's work. You are trying to do too much work yourself. Managers must learn to delegate work.

### The doing-it-the hard-way interruption

Earl is an outstanding teacher of welding in a large technical and vocational school. However, he was recently asked to teach a business course. Earl decided to turn down the assignment, and concentrate on instructing his specialty. Focus your time and effort on work you enjoy and for which you have a reputation for success.

### The spreading-yourself-too-thin interruption

Too many different jobs started at the same time can sap your energy, time, health and accomplishments. Did you ever try to clean out a set of drawers? You start one, you start another, you take time to look over the contents, and, although many are started, few are finished. When you try to accomplish too many jobs at the same time, you're spreading yourself too thin . Start job A, finish it before beginning job B. By the end of the day, you will have completed some important jobs.

### The procrastination interruption

Procrastination is when you delay doing the things you really want to do, secretly hoping you will find the time and opportunity to do them someday. While you are procrastinating, life's important wealth-'TIME'-slips by.

ers prefer to sell their newsletters to businesses rather than to individuals, because businesses are more willing to pay a sizable annual subscription price.

## Newsletter topic ideas

Your newsletter must be well-focused toward a special group. The type of newsletter will be determined by you, after examining what newsletters are available in your field; for example, an entrepreneur from Washington, D.C., after researching publications on federal services and loans, started a newsletter on the numerous services and loans offered by the U.S. government. This newsletter gives a monthly update on the little-known services and opportunities offered by the federal government. In the space provided below, jot down your newsletter topic ideas. Remember that these topics can be based on specialized knowledge, interest, or even a hobby.

| | |
|---|---|
| _____ | _____ |
| _____ | _____ |
| _____ | _____ |
| _____ | _____ |
| _____ | _____ |

Remember to jot down all ideas. No idea is silly, write it down. Make this exercise the beginning of your serious consideration of a successful newsletter. Nothing happens until you make it happen, and the newsletter business is no exception. Review your newspaper and magazines for ideas, and cut them out. Record as many as possible; a few days later go back to the page and add more topics.

## Services are natural newsletter topics

Throughout the 1990s and for many years after the year 2000 the service industries will be taking center stage. Software-writing services, accounting and financial services, medical services, transportation services, temporary employment agencies, craft and art groups, collection agencies, and education and training services are in demand today. How are these special groups getting essential information? Do they have an association? Take the example of Bill Thompson of Maine, who had organized a club for people interested in Model T Fords. To keep his members updated on current and future events, Bill started a newsletter that he is now considering selling to members of Model T Ford clubs all over New England, with later market expansion to include clubs all over the country. Take advantage of the services revolution by examining whether or not your background, interest, and experience can fill a need in one of these areas.

## Brainstorming to get ideas

In modern business practice, small groups brainstorm to develop ideas and solve problems. You may want to choose a friend, your spouse, associate, or neighbor to help you brainstorm to come up with the best newsletter topic. The more ideas you consider, the greater the possibilities.

## Choose a simple newsletter idea in the beginning

Often, beginners in the newsletter business choose a topic that requires far too much research and is too complicated. Some beginners aspire to solve major world problems with their publication. Spirit, enthusiasm, and upbeat attitude are admirable, but you are more likely to succeed with a focused, practical subject. For example, sharpen the focus of a newsletter subject such as *Global Small Business Opportunities in the 1990s* to *Small Business Services.* Redefine the focus of *Elderly Care Worldwide* to *Caring for New England's Elderly.* One newsletter owner redefined her newsletter subject from the far-reaching topic of politics to *Modern Southern Political Strategies,* thus capitalizing on her enthusiasm, resources, and interest as a student of politics with a wide acquaintance among Southern politicians. The key to a successful newsletter topic is making it personal. If you're excited about a subject, you can transfer your interest and excitement to the reader. Avoid choosing a topic with the view of gaining a reputation or earning a large amount of money; if you focus instead on giving your readers the best possible publication for their money, you will succeed.

The alphabetical listing of potential newsletter topics that follows will help you to find the topic that is best for you.

Advertising/public relations
Agriculture
Antiques
Architects
Art/handicrafts
Astrology
Automotive
Banking
Baseball/sports
Beverages
Biology
Blind
Building/construction
Business/economics
Ceramics
Chemistry
Children
Colleges
Communications
Computers/software
Consumer education
Cooking/food service
Correspondence/home study
Criminology and law enforcement
Dance
Dentistry
Design/decoration
Drug abuse/alcoholism
Earth sciences
Education
Energy
Engineering (all fields)
Environmental studies
Ethics
Fire/safety
Fish/fisheries
Flowers/seeds
Food
Gardening
Genealogy
Geography
Gerontology
History
Hobbies (various)
Homosexuality
Hospitals
Hotels/motels/restaurants
Housing
Industrial health and safety
Instruments
Insurance
Interior design and decorating
Jewelry, clocks, and watches
Journalism
Kitchens
Kites
Labor unions
Law
Leather and fur industries
Library and informational
  sciences
Linguistics
Literary and political reviews
Literature
Machinery
Mathematics
Medical sciences
Meetings and Congress
Metallurgy
Meteorology
Metrology and standardization
Military
Mines and mining industry
Motion pictures
Museums and art galleries
Music
Nutrition and dietetics
Occupations and careers
Oriental studies
Packaging
Paints and protective coatings
Paleontology
Paper and pulp

Patents, trademarks, and copyrights
Petroleum and gas
Pharmacy and pharmacology
Philosophy
Photography
Physical fitness and hygiene
Physics
Plastics
Political science
Population studies
Printing
Psychology
Public administration
Public health and safety
Publishing
Quality workplace
Quartz
Real estate
Religion and theology
Rubber
Sciences (comprehensive works)
Shoes and boots
Social sciences (comprehensive works)
Social services and welfare
Sociology
Sound recording and reproduction
Sports and games
Technology (comprehensive works)
Textile industries and fabrics
Theater
Tobacco
Transportation
Travel and tourism
Veterinary science
Water resources
Women's interests
X-rays
Xylophone
Yoga
Youth groups
Zoology

## Research your competition

After you have selected a topic, you need to research whether there are any other newsletters or publications on your subject. Even though a few newsletters or magazines address your potential topic, there might still be a market for your newsletter. Learn as much about the competition as possible.

The *Ulrich's International Periodical Directory,* which can be found at your local library, includes all magazines and journals, and some newsletters, from many countries. The titles are alphabetized according to subject. Entries usually include title, subtitle, sponsoring group, date of origin, frequency of publication, price, editors, publisher, place of publication, the International Standard Serial Number (ISSN), and Dewey decimal classification. An especially useful feature is the list of periodicals that have folded since the previous edition of the directory. *Ulrich's* will show you what periodicals are available, while giving you other ideas for your newsletter topics list.

The *Gale Directory of Newsletters* is another source available in the reference department of your local or regional library. This directory includes newsletters, information services, financial services, associated bulletins, and training and educational services. It lists and briefly describes each newsletter, giving the subject, geographical location, and circulation.

Using these directories will give you a much better idea about what other publications are doing in your subject area. How can you vary the subject, so as to reach a market untouched by the others? How can you treat the subject in a different manner? For example, an enthusiastic newsletter owner in Vermont who wanted to write about wine and spirits found that two not-for-profit (that is, free) newsletters on his subject were available to the public. His strategy was to provide a more varied and in-depth coverage in his newsletter to attract the readers of the free newsletters. Many associations publish not-for-profit newsletters. Check the *Directory of Associations* and the *Gale Directory of Publications* (Figure 2-7) to get more information on these newsletters.

## Potential newsletter markets

Look beyond a newsletter's title, price, and circulation for a moment. Look carefully at the market—the people who will spend their hard-earned money for your newsletter. Your success in this business will depend on matching your newsletter to the best possible market. A good market means people with the purchasing power and desire to subscribe to your newsletter.

Just as brainstorming can produce off-the-wall, unique, impossible, and odd topic ideas, it can develop a creative marketing approach. There are no impossible markets. All ideas are potential winners, as long as you look at them from a different angle—on top, from the left, from the right, and in the middle. The following list gives you an idea of the various markets for your newsletter. Place a check mark next to those that apply to your newsletter.

**★9485★  COLLISION AND TOW AGE**
Kruza Kaleidoscopix Inc.
P.O. Box M
Franklin, MA 02038-0389                 Phone: (617) 528-6211
Magazine on auto body repair and towing in the eastern United States. **Estab.:** 1960. **Frequency:** 9x/yr. **Printing Method:** Offset. **Trim Size:** 8 1/4 x 10 7/8. **No. of Cols. Per Page:** 3. **Col. Width:** 27 nonpareils. **Col. Depth:** 140 agate lines; and **No. of Cols. Per Page:** 2. **Col. Width:** 39 nonpareils. **Col. Depth:** 140 agate lines. **Contacts:** J.A. Kruza, Editor. **ISSN:** 0739-7437. **Subscription:** $13.50.
**Ad Rate:**  BW:    $1,650.00          **Circulation:** Paid ‡19,300
             4C:    $2,647.00                     Controlled ‡4,400

**★9486★  WHEELINGS**
Kruza Kaleidoscopix Inc.
P.O. Box 389
Franklin, MA 02038                     Phone: (617) 528-6211
Tabloid serving manufacturers and jobbers of auto body supplies and larger auto body shops in the United States. **Estab.:** January 1972. **Frequency:** 6x/yr. **Printing Method:** Offset. **Trim Size:** 11 x 17. **No. of Cols. Per Page:** 4. **Col. Width:** 27 nonpareils. **Col. Depth:** 224 agate lines. **Contacts:** J. A. Kruza, Editor. **Subscription:** $11.00 for 3 years.
**Ad Rate:**  BW:    $750.00            **Circulation:** Paid ‡4,900
                                                    Non-paid ‡13,000
Color advertising accepted.

### GARDNER (G2), pop. 17,900.

Worcester Co. (C). 58 m W of Boston. Chair city of the world. Environmental control systems, molded plastics, foundry and machine shop products, steel & metal tubing, yarn. Dairy farms.

**★9487★  THE NEWS**
309 Central St.
Gardner, MA 01440                      Phone: (617) 632-8000
Newspaper. **Estab.:** 1869. **Frequency:** Daily (eve.) except Sun. **Printing Method:** Offset. **No. of Cols. Per Page:** 8. **Col. Width:** 21 nonpareils. **Col. Depth:** 301 agate lines. **Contacts:** Maria Shersnow, Editor; C. Gordon Bell, Publisher; James Murphy, Advertising Manager. **Subscription:** $63.00.
**Ad Rate:**  GLR:    $.30              **Circulation:** ★9,187

### GLOUCESTER (M2), pop. 27,768.

Essex Co. (NE). 28 m NE of Boston, on S side of Cape Ann Peninsula. Summer resort. Chief industry is catching, canning, freezing and shipping of fish, especially cod, haddock, halibut, mackerel and ocean perch. Glue, nets and seines, ink, isinglass, cod liver oil, oiled clothing, paint, wooden boxes, sportswear manufactured.

**★9488★  MINI, THE MAGAZINE FOR IBM 34/36/38 DECISION MAKERS**
Para Research, Inc.
85 Eastern Ave.
Gloucester, MA 01930                   Phone: (617) 283-3438
For nontechnical decision makers responsible for IBM System 34/36/or/38. **Estab.:** February 1984. **Frequency:** Quarterly. **Printing Method:** 8 3/8 x 10 7/8. **Web. No. of Cols. Per Page:** 3. **Contacts:** Frank D. Molinski, Publisher; Marlene Comet, General Director. **Subscription:** $16.00 annually; two-year subscriptions are $32.00.
                                       **Circulation:** Non-paid 34,000
Contact publisher for ad information. List of qualified subscribers maintained in-house.

**★9489★  MUSICIAN MAGAZINE**
31 Commerical St.
P.O. Box 701
Gloucester, MA 01930                   Phone: (617) 281-3110
Music magazine. **Estab.:** 1976. **Frequency:** Monthly. **Printing Method:** Offset. **No. of Cols. Per Page:** 3. **Col. Width:** 27 nonpareils. **Col. Depth:** 140 agate lines; and **No. of Cols. Per Page:** 2. **Col. Width:** 42 nonpareils. **Col. Depth:** 142 agate lines. **Contacts:** Jonathan Baird, Editor; Gordon Baird, Publisher; Gary Krasner, Advertising Manager. **Subscription:** $20.00.
**Ad Rate:**  BW:    $3,940.00         **Circulation:** ★100,585
             4C:    $4,990.00

**★9490★  TIMES**
Whittemore St.
Gloucester, MA 01930                   Phone: (617) 283-7000
Newspaper. **Estab.:** 1857. **Frequency:** Daily (eve.) except Sun. **Printing Method:** Offset. **No. of Cols. Per Page:** 8. **Col. Width:** 22 nonpareils. **Col. Depth:** 294 agate lines. **Contacts:** William McCulloch, Editor; Frank O. King, Publisher. **Subscription:** $45.00.
                                       **Circulation:** ★11,662

### GREAT BARRINGTON (A4), pop. 7,405.

Berkshire Co. (W). On Housatonic River, 20 m SW of Pittsfield. Summer resort. Pine timber. Paper mills; Log homes. Nuclear components. Dairy, poultry farms.

**★9491★  BERKSHIRE COURIER**
P.O. Box 150
Great Barrington, MA 01230            Phone: (413) 528-3020
Newspaper. **Estab.:** 1834. **Frequency:** Weekly (Thurs.). **Printing Method:** Offset. **No. of Cols. Per Page:** 7. **Col. Width:** 19 nonpareils. **Col. Depth:** 294 agate lines. **Contacts:** Bernard Drew, Editor; John Larabee, Publisher. **Subscription:** $13.00.
**Ad Rate:**  GLR:    $.29             **Circulation:** 5,450

**★9492★  RESEARCH REPORTS**
American Institute for Economic Research
Division St.
Great Barrington, MA 01230            Phone: (413) 528-1216
Economics newsletter. **Estab.:** 1933. **Frequency:** Semimonthly. **Printing Method:** Offset. **No. of Cols. Per Page:** 2. **Col. Width:** 40 nonpareils. **Col. Depth:** 140 agate lines. **Contacts:** Robert A. Gilmour, Editor. **ISSN:** 0034-5407. **Subscription:** $48.00.
                                       **Circulation:** Paid ‡8,000
                                                    Non-paid ‡200

**★9493★  SOUTHERN BERKSHIRE SHOPPER'S GUIDE**
35 Bridge St.
P.O. Box 89
Great Barrington, MA 01230            Phone: (413) 528-0095
Shopper. **Estab.:** April 15, 1968. **Frequency:** Weekly (Tues.). **Printing Method:** Offset. **No. of Cols. Per Page:** 6. **Col. Width:** 224 agate lines. **Contacts:** Eunice Raifstanger, Editor. John T. Raifstanger, Publisher; Robin Hare, Advertising Manager.
**Ad Rate:**  BW:    $336.00           **Circulation:** Paid ‡16,047
             PCI:   $3.50                           Free ‡6,500

### GREENFIELD† (D2), pop. 18,436.

Franklin Co. (NW). On Connecticut River, 20 m N of Northampton. Manufactures taps, dies, machine tools, grinding and finishing machinery, sterling silver tableware, shovels, rakes, paper boxes. Agriculture. Corn, cucumbers, squash, cabbage, apples, potatoes.

**★9494★  THE RECORDER**
14 Hope St.
P.O. Box 273
Greenfield, MA 01301                  Phone: (413) 772-0261
Local newspaper. **Estab.:** February 1, 1792. **Frequency:** Mon-Sat (eve.). **Printing Method:** Offset. **Trim Size:** 13 3/4 x 22 3/4. **No. of Cols. Per Page:** 6. **Col. Width:** 26 nonpareils. **Col. Depth:** 298 agate lines. **Contacts:** Tim Blagg, Editor; Al Hutchison, Publisher; Mark A. Iacuessa, Advertising Manager. **Subscription:** $87.00.
**Ad Rate:**  GLR:    $.614            **Circulation:** ★15,384
             BW:     $1,102.95
             4C:     $1,447.95
             PCI:    $8.60
Member of Newspapers of New England, Inc.

**★9495★  TOWN CRIER**
47 Main St.
P.O. Box 1031
Greenfield, MA 01302                  Phone: (413) 774-7226
Local newspaper. **Estab.:** 1967. **Frequency:** Weekly (Wed.). **Printing Method:** Offset. **No. of Cols. Per Page:** 7. **Col. Width:** 20 nonpareils. **Col. Depth:** 192 agate lines. **Contacts:** Nancy Landue, Editor; Donald W. Lamson, Publisher and Advertising Manager. **Subscription:** $13.50.
**Ad Rate:**  BW:    $470.40           **Circulation:** Free 20,825
             4C:    $680.40

### HAMILTON (L2), pop. 6,960.

Essex Co (NE) 3 m NE of Wenham. Residential.

**★9496★  GRAY'S SPORTING JOURNAL**
205 Willow St.
Hamilton, MA 01982                    Phone: (508) 468-4486
Hunting and fishing magazine. **Estab.:** 1975. **Frequency:** 4x/yr. **Printing Method:** Offset. **Trim Size:** 8 1/8 x 10 7/8. **No. of Cols. Per Page:** 2. **Col. Width:** 35 nonpareils. **Col. Depth:** 143 agate lines. **Contacts:** Edward Gray, Editor; Rebecca Gray, Publisher; Susan Brophy, Advertising Manager. **Subscription:** $26.50, $6.95 single issue.
**Ad Rate:**  BW:    $1,460.00         **Circulation:** Paid ‡35,000
             4C:    $1,960.00                      Non-paid ‡1,000

### HANOVER (L4), pop. 11,358.

Plymouth Co. (SE) 30 m S. of Boston. Residential.

**★9497★  SOUTH SHORE NEWS**
One Mayflower Dr.
Hanover, MA 02339                     Phone: (617) 878-5100
Newspaper. **Estab.:** 1859. **Frequency:** Weekly (Mon.). **Printing Method:** Offset. **No. of Cols. Per Page:** 6. **Col. Width:** 21 nonpareils. **Col. Depth:** 224 agate lines. **Contacts:** Joanne Dotton, Editor and Publisher. **Subscription:** $30.00.
**Ad Rate:**  GLR:    $.86             **Circulation:** 73,003

### HATFIELD (D3), pop. 3,045.

Hampshire Co. (WC) 9 m E of Williamburg. Residential.

**★9498★  VALLEY ADVOCATE**
87 School St.
Hatfield, MA 01038                    Phone: (413) 247-9301
Newspaper. **Estab.:** 1973. **Frequency:** Weekly (Wed.). **Printing Method:** Offset. **No. of Cols. Per Page:** 4. **Col. Width:** 224 nonpareils. **Col. Depth:** 224 agate lines. **Contacts:** Christine Austin, Editor; Geoffrey A. Robinson and Christine Austin, Publishers; Mitch Young, Advertising Manager. **Subscription:** $30.00.
**Ad Rate:**  GLR:    $1.71            **Circulation:** Free 70,000
Prints editions for Greenfield, Northhampton, and Greater Springfield.

**Rates**—(GLR) general line rate; (BW) one-time black & white page rate; (4C) one-time four color page rate; (SAU) standard advertising unit rate; (CNU) Canadian newspaper advertising unit rate; (PCI) per column inch rate.
**Circulation**—★=A.B.C. Statement; ●=C.C.A.B. Qualified Audit; ♦=C.A.C. Audit; ±=V.A.C. Statement; >=B.P.A. Audit; ‡=Publisher's Report; §=P.O. Statement; Bold face figures=sworn; Light figures=estimated.

*Fig. 2-7. A page from the* Gale Directory of Publications.

_____ Mail-order owners
_____ Small-business owners
_____ Engineers
_____ Teachers
_____ Nurses
_____ Buyers of business books
_____ Insurance salespeople
_____ Home economics teachers
_____ Chemical engineers
_____ Corn farmers
_____ Publishing houses
_____ Guidance counselors
_____ Do-it-yourselfers
_____ Graphic artists
_____ Salespeople in the computer field

_____ Gift store owners
_____ Working women
_____ Accountants
_____ Left-handed people
_____ Doctors
_____ Attendees of stress management seminars
_____ Computer/VCR owners
_____ Business colleges
_____ Civil engineers
_____ Printers
_____ Convenience stores
_____ Handicapped people
_____ Gourmet cooks
_____ Female lawyers
_____ Buyers of expensive jewelry

You can rent mailing lists for many markets from a mailing-list company. These markets can also be reached by advertising in specific magazines. For example, you can reach 200,000 to 300,000 writers by placing an advertisement in either *The Writer Magazine* or the *Writer's Digest.*

## Putting your newsletter and market together

Now that you have reviewed and checked the applicable markets for your newsletter, let's join the forces. Continue the following listing, first jotting down your topic idea and then matching it to the most likely market. Use as many ideas as you can from your topic and market ideas lists.

| *Newsletter topics* | *Markets* |
|---|---|
| Accounting newsletter (A) | (A) Accountants |
| Penny stocks investment newsletter (B) | (A) C.P.A. firms |
| _____ | (A) Public accountants |
| _____ | (B) Other penny stock newsletter subscribers |
| _____ | (B) Small investors |
| _____ | _____ |
| _____ | _____ |
| _____ | _____ |
| _____ | _____ |
| _____ | _____ |
| _____ | _____ |
| _____ | _____ |
| _____ | _____ |
| _____ | _____ |
| _____ | _____ |
| _____ | _____ |
| _____ | _____ |
| _____ | _____ |

# Target your newsletter to a specific market

Sell your newsletter on sports to sports fans, and your professional baseball newsletter to baseball fans rather than all sports fans. Sell your newsletter on raising twins to the parents of twins. Your target market must have something in common, must be identified in a list or a directory, and must have a need and the money to purchase your newsletter. Your target market also must be large enough for you to make a profit on your publication. A profit is the difference between your total sales—let's say $75,000 a year—and your total expenses from, for example, printing, mailing, and advertising—a total of $50,000—yielding a $25,000 profit. Your goal will be to keep the sales high enough to cover expenses and earn a profit. A large target market will help you increase your profit and expand your business.

# Get to know your market

A newsletter owner in Washington writes a monthly, 8-page newsletter for writers of nonfiction books and articles, and to keep this market satisfied requires new ideas, techniques, and opportunities each month. The owner knows the needs of the market because he has been a writer for many years and shares many of his readers' fears, goals, and aspirations. His newsletter offers hope, insight, and inspiration.

It helps to have the same occupation as your target reader, but you can learn more about any market by reading the same magazines, watching the same television programs, sharing their entertainment, becoming a part of their lives. Once you publish a few issues you will receive letters back from readers—some positive, some negative. Accept praise, but listen carefully to criticism; you may learn from it. You can learn more about your market by defining it as much as possible. One way to segment your market is by using its statistics or demographics, as in the following example:

| | |
|---|---|
| Sex | Female |
| Age | 25–35 |
| Race | White |
| Marital status | 40% married; 60% single |
| Income | $30,000 annually |

Occupation            Professional/business
Geographic location   Urban

Remember, your newsletter topic must be selected with your market in mind; consider the time it will take to bring the two together. What does your market need?—a publication that offers the latest information on the stock market, or on economic trends, or on gerontology, or on drug abuse in America, or on new ways to communicate by using cable television, or on choosing a college or university in the 1990s. The market needs information that it cannot get from its association newsletter or other sources. Match the topic to your target market.

## Face your competition

You have competition, and it will require a full knowledge of this competition to succeed. Magazines, seminars, small-business workshops, reports, business courses, technical classes, talk radio programs, television programs, audio/video cassettes, computer software, and other newsletters may address your market. Take time to review your competition to see whether it is serious. How do you know if the competition is serious? By looking at the circulation of a newsletter, for example, and at its content. Why start a newsletter if you are going to rehash material already published by a competitor? You will defeat your own idea. Why does your competition have a circulation? What are they doing to keep this circulation? Does your competition focus on one area to the neglect of others? Does your competition keep its focus issue after issue, year after year? Too often, newsletters start with a clear focus but lose it—and their circulation.

## Compete by using a different stance

A boxer in the ring can outmaneuver his opponent by changing his stance, throwing his opponent off guard, confusing him, and proceeding until victory is at hand. In the newsletter business you can take a different stance in your approach to the market. such as when you find an interest that is quite broad, for example, energy, and the competition fails to address solar energy, you might have a good newsletter topic. How about a newsletter on speech therapy for adults? When the newsletters and magazines lack current news about this important area, you again may have an excellent topic idea. Find the need, make certain you are interested enough in the subject to pursue it, and then develop a strategy to reach it.

## Choosing a winning name for your newsletter

Your newsletter title must communicate your message and get attention. It must be a name that means something to the target market. For example, let's say that your newsletter topic is legislation that can affect the 50,000 chiropractors in the country; you might want to call it *The Chiropractors' Government Newsletter*. The name shows that you are writing with an important viewpoint from Washington, D.C. Another approach is to call the newsletter a report, for example, *Penny Stock Advisory Report*, a title that shows the topics and what you're trying to do—report and advise the subscribers on penny stocks.

Give yourself enough time to get the best possible name. Throw out many ideas, and write them down on the following lines.

_____    _____

_____    _____

_____    _____

_____    _____

_____    _____

Once you select the five or six best names, put them to a vote to determine the best. Another approach is to write a sales letter describing the newsletter and asking for the subscriptions or orders. Send out 100 letters using the name *Penny Stock Advisory Report*, and 100 letters using the name *Penny Stock Newsletter*, and chart the results. Let's say you get four orders for the *Penny Stock Advisory Report* and only one order for *Penny Stock Newsletter*. You can make your decision on your name, and then contact the customers who subscribed to the name you discontinued, giving them the new name.

For more newsletter name ideas, review the names of newsletters below:

*New Career Ways*
*Speech Therapy Letter*
*Fringe Benefits Forecaster*

*The Gallagher Report*

*The Home-Based Mail-Order Report*

*Selling Information Newsletter*

*Telephone Communications Newsletter*

*Baseball Cards News*

*The Vegetarian Report*

*The Bartender's Letter*

You might consider adding a subtitle to your newsletter to give people more information about its content. The newsletter titles and suggested newsletter titles below will give you ideas:

*New Career Ways*

*Suggested subtitle:* New ideas to increase your success at work

*The Gallagher Report*

A confidential letter to management, marketing, and advertising executives

*Selling Information Newsletter*

Getting your information marketed successfully

*Home-Based Mail-Order Report*

How to start, operate, and manage a mail-order operation at home

Strive for a name that is easy to remember and describes what the reader will receive. Keep working on your newsletter name until you get it just right. There is a large payoff in using a strong name.

## Summary

This chapter lays the foundation for your successful newsletter business. It is important to choose an appropriate topic for your newsletter and tie the topic to your proposed market. Your market is a group of people who have the purchasing power and the desire to buy your publication. Your newsletter must be special, with information unavailable in other publications or communication outlets. Read other newsletters and magazines. Consider service areas such as accounting, transportation, communication, and the computer in your search for a newsletter topic. Research your topic well and match it to the market. Target and know your market. Face competition head on. Choose a winning name.

Now let's discuss how to make your newsletter essential reading.

# 3

# Making your newsletter essential reading

A successful newsletter is the result of choosing a good topic, targeting a market, and making your newsletter essential reading for that market. You never get a second chance to make the best first impression. Today's competition is fierce, and to compete and win requires a sharp focus on your goals.

## Do you sell or entertain your customer?

I have a friend in the music business, who sells musical products and also plays them. His shop is located in a busy shopping area, and lately he has been focusing more on entertaining than on selling. Entertaining is important, but delivering information will sell your newsletter. You will succeed when you focus on *selling* your newsletter.

A mail-order jewelry business cannot survive by selling one ring to Sarah M. in Arizona; it must sell Sarah many rings, and bracelets, necklaces, and earrings over the years.

You, in turn, want life-long customers for your *newsletter*. Your most important goal will be to make your newsletter essential reading, so that your subscribers will renew their subscriptions year after year. Renewals are the fuel that keeps your newsletter business running. They result from supplying your readers with a publication they need and want. In simple terms, readers want to get their money's worth from your product. How do you give them the most for their money? *By knowing what people want!* Give people what they want on a steady basis and you'll be well on your way to success.

## Write a mission statement

Let's say you want to publish a national newsletter for bartenders. A call to the reference librarian of the local public library tells you there are 400,000 eating and drinking establishments in the United States, which are listed in the *Statistical Abstract of the United States.* This reference is published by the U.S. Bureau of Census. Your research also shows that there are *four* newsletters, and at least one magazine, presently directed to this audience. After examining the competition, you decide to start a newsletter that offers advice on giving bar patrons top-quality service. Before you publish your first issue, or even do further planning, write a mission statement. A *mission statement* is a well-thought-out plan of what you want to accomplish. It gives you direction, and it shows you what paths you want to take to reach your goal. A mission statement is similar to a New Year's resolution, in which you promise to do something, or change your behavior in a particular manner. The mission statement in the newsletter business is a contract you write with yourself to expand on the standards and focus of your newsletter. After each issue comes out, review the mission statement to see whether or not your product is living up to its original charter. When you find your newsletter straying away from your mission statement, stop the process, review it, and get back on track. Review the following mission statement:

My newsletter's primary goal is to offer a publication with advice on how to give quality information to bar patrons.

*Description of newsletter.*   Quality bar service is a process. I will do my level best to help my readers achieve a high standard of service.

*Most important newsletter content.*   My newsletter content will cover three general areas:

- Customer service
- Retaining customers
- Modern selling principles

*Methods to obtain subscriptions and renewals.*  My newsletter renewals will result from my enthusiasm and discipline, my machinery, my employees, and my ability to measure my performance regularly and make the necessary changes to maintain my standards and focus.

I want 5000 subscribers within two years.

This mission statement is a contract to focus on your basic goal and your commitment to your market. Never forget why you wanted to start the newsletter in the first place. When you find yourself veering off course, move back to your original premise.

During a recent newsletter seminar, a lawyer expressed interest in doing a newsletter on how middle- and low-income people could either hire lawyers or decide to handle their own cases. I advised this seminar attendee to put these ideas into her mission statement. Another seminar attendee wanted to start a newsletter on computer services for small businesses. I asked him to fill out a mission statement, fully describing the project at hand.

Use a format such as the following to describe your own goals:

*Description of newsletter:*  ————————————————

*Most important newsletter content:*  ——————————————

*Methods to obtain renewals:*  —————————————————

Read and reread your mission statement daily, so that you know exactly what is needed to get started successfully. The mission statement sets the groundwork for a firm foundation for your newsletter business.

## Write a golden contract with your subscribers

Many companies have slogans that start something like this: "The quality goes in...." Or, "We care about you...." These themes give a particular perception of the product to the customer and can be thought of as "golden contracts" of a sort. *Your* golden contract is important in keeping a customer on your subscription list month after month, year after year. Your contract is not written; it is unspoken, but it is essential to your success. The golden contract means that you understand your customers' rights, and that one of these rights is the expectation of a quality publication. Customers will expect you to remember what you listed in your mission statement and your promotional mailings, and in your other communications as well. The golden contract means that you respect your customers and never take their rights for granted. When you take customers for granted, your competitors will have new subscribers. The following are important rights each newsletter subscriber should expect.

1. The right to a quality newsletter.
2. The right to expect the newsletter to keep a clear focus on the information that the customer wants and needs for success.
3. The right to complain when the product is not acceptable.
4. The right to cancel when the product fails.
5. The right to cancel when the newsletter fails to deliver what you said it would.
6. In the event of cancellation, the right to expect a refund for the unused subscription, or some mutually agreeable adjustment.
7. The right to expect you to communicate promptly when there is a problem.
8. The right to be treated fairly in all dealings with you.

Today's consumer is tough, is well aware of other products, will cancel or change products quickly, and will give you loyalty only when you earn it. Since today's consumers are very hard to sell in the first place, it is even more difficult to convince them to renew. The golden contract means that you know where you want to go, and that you're willing to do the work necessary to stay on focus so as to deliver the best.

When you develop your campaign to get newsletter subscriptions (see Chapter 11), you might want to refer to your mission statement and your customers' bill of rights. Will Rogers, speaking at a business luncheon in New York City, was asked, "How can you reach success in life?" Will turned slowly and said; "Know what you're doing, love what you're doing, and believe in what you're doing." These simple but profound words aptly describe what is necessary, not only to start your newsletter successfully, but to bring it to the top.

Let's return to *The Bartender's Letter* example. Let's say that your subscribers bought *The Bartender's Letter* because they believed that it could help them. Your mission statement and your golden contract worked; now you've got to do the *hard* work of maintaining the quality of the product and of customer service that will keep your customer buying from you. Each time you do something right and show your customers that you are committed to them, your chances of getting their friends, associates, and relatives to subscribe increases substantially.

## Develop strategies for your newsletter

The mission statement is an overview of your goal and the paths you will take to achieve it. The golden contract is your awareness of the rights of your subscribers. It is difficult to please today's media-glutted customer. You must be tough to get the business. The best way to do this is to develop strategies to complement your mission statement and your golden contract. As you develop your strategies for *The Bartender's Letter* ask yourself if they tie into and contribute to your mission statement and your golden contract.

This dedication to a mission statement and a golden contract may be the most important advice in this book. My experience in the newsletter and publishing business is that hundreds, even thousands, of newsletters start with a strong objective and a worthwhile idea. Too often, for a number of reasons, the owner's attention becomes diverted to other areas that are unrelated to the original purpose of the newsletter. The mission statement of *The Bartender's Letter* states that the focus will be on quality bar service, retaining bar customers, and selling services, and will avoid subjects outside this area.

Focus on your main target. Like a person at a rifle range, direct your aim toward the middle of the target. A good strategy would be to set up an editorial calendar for a monthly newsletter, assigning a subject to each month. A sample editorial calendar follows.

| Month | Projected Topic | Actual Topic |
|---|---|---|
| January | Principles of Quality Service | |
| February | Quality Service Worldwide | |
| March | Why Customers Buy Services | |
| April | Sales Professionals | |
| May | Keeping Customers Returning and Buying | |
| June | Customer Demographics | |
| July | Communication in Marketing | |
| August | Results of Bartenders' Convention | |
| September | Success Secrets of Top Bartenders | |
| October | Psychographics | |
| November | Testing Your Selling | |
| December | Quality during Holidays | |

By reviewing your editorial calendar you can plan your newsletter issues to avoid duplication. The editorial calendar is just a guide; you can change it in response to changes in government regulations or to economic changes such as recessions, inflation, or tax increases or cuts. A successful newsletter has structure, but it also has built-in flexibility to meet changing needs.

In *A Raisin in the Sun*, Walter Lee Younger says to his son, "I'll hand you the world." *You* will have the world at your fingertips when you direct your strategies to meet the needs of your customers. Look at your product with your customer's eyes. See how your newsletter can help others.

One strategy that will help make your newsletter required reading is the evaluation sheet, which you should prepare before your first issue. How your customer will grade your newsletter will determine whether or not you will get the renewal. The following is an example of an evaluation sheet:

1. Is the newsletter personal to you?

2. Do you enjoy the newsletter? Was it punctual?

3. Is it easy to read and understand?

4. Is it attractive and eye catching?

5. Do you receive new information and useful ideas regularly?

6. Does it live up to your original expectation upon signing up for the newsletter?

7. Is the newsletter giving you entertainment or information? Which one, and please answer why?

8. Is the newsletter of sufficient quality for you to sign a renewal notice or continue the subscription?

I recall the evaluations I used at my college seminars. At the end of the semester, I would hand them out for the students to evaluate the course and my instruction. The idea was a good one; certain connections could be made once the evaluations were read and analyzed. By reading the evaluations before the beginning of the following semester I could understand better what was expected from me in the course.

The newsletter evaluation above puts you at a definite advantage over other newsletter owners because you will know what future subscribers will expect from you. You will know how you will be judged before you begin your business. The evaluation can help you avoid a series of cancellations or slow renewals. The key question in the evaluation is item 8, which asks whether the newsletter is of sufficient quality to earn a renewal for another year. Focus on quality to succeed. Fill out an evaluation statement yourself on a regular basis. Put yourself in the shoes of your customers. Would you continue to read and pay for this newsletter? Be honest with the most important person—*yourself!*

## Treat everyone fairly

This may be the strategy that will make you a winner. Be objective about the stories you cover and the people you will interview, and be enthusiastic while staying close to your mission statement. Avoid giving subscribers, companies, or organizations special treatment. Treat your customer the way you would like to be treated as the customer—fairly and above board at all times.

I don't recommend accepting advertisements for your newsletter. Advertisement is a paid form of nonpersonal presentation of goods and service by an identified sponsor. An advertisement or two in your newsletter, even if the advertisement is yours, clearly breaks ethical guidelines. For example, a New England newsletter owner targeting small business owners decided to accept advertisements to help defray costs during the first year. Once he accepted these advertisements, he fell into the trap of slanting his editorial content to the advertisers' benefit rather than keeping it objective. Or, let's say you are writing a newsletter on investments, giving your readers important information on the best ways to invest their money. One of your recent issues has advertisements on mutual funds and penny stocks. What is this stating to the customers? Is it informing them that mutual funds and penny stocks are the way to invest today? Producing a quality newsletter without advertisements will bring you enough revenue; there is no need to let someone purchase special consideration.

Don't give special favors just because you received a subscription from a company. Your editorial content is not for sale to anyone for any price, gift, favor, or recognition. For example, let's say your energy newsletter is focusing on efforts to clean up toxic waste. You check your subscription list and you find that a company or organization who has been a toxic waste abuser is your customer. Do you stop future issues dealing with the toxic waste issue? No, you continue to discuss openly all the issues important to the subscribers, issue after issue, year after year. When you try to give one person or group special attention, you jeopardize all your other subscribers. Publish the best newsletter possible for all your readers, and you will succeed.

## Be creative

An important strategy to further set you apart is to be as creative as possible based on the competition in your field. For example, a New England engineer with an interest in boating wants to put out a newsletter on boating tips. He targets boat owners who take a number of boating trips during the year. His newsletter will include information unavailable to this market in books, videos, and other newsletters.

Creativity can help you reach a specialized market. A newsletter devoted exclusively to chocolates, printed on chocolate-colored paper, arrives in the mail imbued with chocolate scent. The owner includes information on frozen chocolate mousse, truffles, and chocolate cake, and interviews celebrities who are chocolate lovers. Be willing to add the content required to keep your readers interested and renewing.

Be creative, not only in the way you write your newsletter, but in your selection of your market. For example, Karen from Ohio started a newsletter that offers marketing advice for small businesses; she is now trying to reach the market in England and Ireland. A newsletter is a unique opportunity to select a market anywhere in the country, even the world.

Another idea was Harry's for a Florida-based newsletter on career management that presents hard-to-get information to help people plan, operate, and set workable strategies to move ahead. The newsletter interviews successful managers who know how to position themselves in a favorable career direction. The ideas and techniques presented in this newsletter can be used by a person right out of school or one who has been working for many years. The newsletter presents the career as a business or profit center, and offers material for personnel managers, schools, placement centers, managers, and individuals interested in improving their success at work.

Still another idea is Sheila's newsletter on her favorite hobby: community theater. Sheila has spent the last 12 years of her life as a director, choreographer, set designer, costume designer, lighting technician, and photographer for her local community theater. She's also written advertising and done promotion. In short, Sheila had some well-rounded experience to offer her readers. Her market will be the many community theaters all over the country. Sheila is now working on her mission statement and researching her target market; she hopes to start publishing soon. You too can choose a topic that fits interests, skills, and experience.

## Summary

Making your newsletter essential reading requires a well-written mission statement of your editorial intent and your strategy for obtaining subscriptions and renewals. The mission statement will become very important to you in marketing your newsletter. The golden contract with your subscribers identifies their rights as customers. Give them the best quality possible, as well as excellent customer service. Your reputation will depend on how you treat your customers. Develop a clear set of strategies. Strategies are easier to develop when the topic

is meaningful and personal to you. Many successful newsletter owners do an annual editorial calendar to plan for the year. Give your
customers what they need to be better at what they do. Do not accept
advertising for your newsletter. Be objective in your choice of content. Be creative in the way you look at your newsletter and your market.

Now let's discuss how you can choose the best possible content.

# 4

# Choosing a winning content

Winning content is essential for a successful newsletter. Your content is the subjects, topics, and elements included in your newsletter. Your customers will judge each issue primarily on its content. Like food product ingredients, which are listed on the label, newsletter "ingredients" must include quality items, or the customer will buy a competitor's product the next time. Remember, the more you know about your product—your newsletter topic—the easier it will be to choose the best possible content.

## You're the editorial and marketing manager

You have power as the owner of your own newsletter. You determine what goes into it. You are not at the mercy of someone else who will make the final determination of what material, emphasis, or special theme will be used. Use that power by writing only the most important information available in the field today. Quality copy sells! When you have focused on the best newsletter copy, and delivered it, you will be ready to replace your editorial hat with the marketing manager's hat. Give your market your best, and it will be easier to sell. As marketing manager you can sell by presenting your past, present, and future issues—the content.

Choose only the best content. When going on a boat trip, you bring only the essential tools, the equipment necessary to complete the trip successfully; excessive weight will cause your boat to sink. The same principle applies to newsletters. Feature only the content that will satisfy your customers. Before an issue of a newspaper is published a meeting is held to decide which articles will appear. Some articles will be put aside for another issue. In book publishing, an editorial board votes on the book proposals for the coming year. In your newsletter business, you are the editorial board, and you determine which material will be used.

## Become an expert in your field

You can make the best decisions on content when you are an expert in your field, so take steps to become one. If your newsletter is on wines, and you are not expert in this area but would like to be, simply work hard to learn the field. Having a thorough knowledge of wines will help you to write with authority and gain a strong following. Visit vineyards. See how the wine is processed. Learn how climate, soil, and fertilizer affect wine quality. Study the history of wine production. Find out the technology relevant to this field. Read about wine in magazines, newsletters, and newspapers. Talk to people who work in the wineries and to those in the boardrooms of the top wine producers. Go to wine tastings. Become an expert by putting in the time and effort.

You can start your newsletter while being an expert-in-training by hiring an expert to work with you until you get your sea legs. You may want to have the expert write the newsletter, or you can ask your expert to review it. You make the final decision on any changes that your expert suggests.

## Use the theme of your mission statement

Your content theme will be in your mission statement (see Chapter 3), and when you review your issue content, make sure that it reflects this theme. An energy newsletter featuring ways to save energy and the Earth uses the theme of monitoring the consumption of gasoline, electricity, and water. A security newsletter uses the theme of practical approaches to keeping businesses and people safe from harm. A consultant's newsletter is to help subscribers run their businesses profitably in the 1990s. An executive search newsletter's theme is the placement of unemployed executives.

## Be original

Try to carve out an editorial content that sets your newsletter apart from the competition. An innovative approach can assure you market share. The power of innovation is illustrated by the following anecdote:

> A wealthy woman asked a famous millinery designer to design a hat for her. He placed a canvas form on her head, and in eight minutes, with a single piece of ribbon, he created a beautiful hat right before her eyes.
>
> The matron was delighted. "How much will that be?," she asked.
>
> "Fifty dollars," he replied.
>
> "Why, that's outrageous," she said, "It's only a piece of ribbon!"
>
> The milliner quickly unraveled the ribbon and, handing it to her, said, "Madame, the ribbon is free!"
>
> ABIGAIL VAN BUREN

Communicate your carefully selected content creatively. *Do it your way!*

## Choose a content formula

Choose a content formula based on your mission statement and your experience. Visualize your customer at home:

What is he or she expecting from your newsletter?

How will this issue help your customer?

Can your customer use the material immediately?

Is the news current and relevant to the customer's needs?

Present what the customer needs to succeed. Your customer is paying you a handsome fee for your best content, not your second best. Like the person on the boat trip who screens all equipment before it is permitted into the boat, you must screen your contents. For example, a prospective newsletter owner in New Jersey is considering addressing the rights of disabled veterans, and will focus on legislation affecting veterans; veterans' health care, relief programs, and benefits; scholarships for veterans and their children; and discrimination based on the disability. These issues are important to her target market and must be addressed for the newsletter to succeed. Leave less important issues for other media, such as radio, television, or the newspapers.

A recent issue of a consulting newsletter featured an article on governmental organizations, and included a note from the publisher, an article on matching consultants to clients, a section on consultants in the news, a survey of independent consultants, tips on relaxation techniques, an article on group insurance, and a book review section. Some content elements to consider for your newsletter are listed below.

Note from publisher

Table of contents

Feature article

Legislation affecting subscribers

Promotions and people in the news

News in the field

Specialized information on customer service

New products and services

Surveys in the field

Formulas, graphs, and charts

Book reviews

New ideas in the field

Success stories

Some newsletters have a section that features new products and services. Once you issue your first newsletter, you will receive news releases on new products or services. News releases are statements, sometimes but not always accompanied by a photograph, about the facts and figures, features, and devices of the new product or service.

News releases don't try to sell you the product or service; they give only the basic facts about the product or service. Although a two-page news release may be sent, only a small section is finally printed. Many newsletters will publish only a sentence or two about a product or service. You must decide whether you will allow your valuable space to be used for new products or service information. As an aside, newsletters also inform their readers about new newsletters. In your marketing plan, consider sending a news release and a copy of your newsletter to other newsletters, asking that they print your address. A Massachusetts home-based owner included his address right in his newsletter title to get this free promotion.

## Don't include too many elements of content

If you present too many subjects, you *may* not give them all sufficient coverage. For example, if you want to devote a large part of your issue to the newly passed federal bill, The Americans with Disabilities Act, and how it will impact on American businesses, especially on personnel departments, allow sufficient space to do the subject justice. A recent issue of a small-business newsletter shortchanged this subject, quickly shifting gears into the subject of seminars for customers. The shift disoriented readers and gave insufficient information on both disabilities and the seminars.

## Learn from your mistakes

It is useful to review two or three past issues in order to view the newsletter objectively. Is the content specialized enough to help your customers? The answer to this question not only will help you to select the best possible content for the current issue, but will open up new ideas for future issues. One newsletter owner decided to start a newsletter for accountants with information on the field, and on general management skills. After the first year, renewals and new subscriptions began to fall off. The newsletter owner reviewed her last six issues and noticed that the content was too general, and that some of the material overlapped. There was a lack of specialized information in the publications; to help the newsletter survive she included information on changing accounting standards and the latest developments from the national accounting boards. Since making these changes, there have been increased subscriptions and renewals, and customers are calling and writing with favorable comments.

## Don't make excessive content changes

You will receive requests to add different columns to your newsletter. Listen to all ideas, but be cautious in implementing them. For example, a subscriber from Washington asks you about covering more surveys, a Florida subscriber wants to know more about corporate promotions, a Minnesota subscriber wants information on customer service skills. You cannot satisfy all these requests. Make changes when you deem them necessary, but remember not to make excessive content changes, because you may end up confusing your customers. Make each inch count.

*Don't worry about getting the perfect content formula when you start your newsletter.* Some newsletters begin by sending out trade information to their customers who are members of clubs or organizations. After a number of issues, an understanding of the market and an excitement about the material combine to develop a content formula. Present what you feel is the most appropriate content. As you progress, you will develop the content mixture that is right for you and your customers.

## The one person's opinion newsletter

The one person's opinion approach is good for someone who is well established and well known in a particular field or discipline. Your main problem will be the ability to publish long enough to get established. This type of newsletter is a natural, for example, for a mutual funds expert that retired on top, with an impressive record for handling investments. Customers will want to know the formula for success, and will pay for specific opinions on how to earn more money with their investments. Use this approach when your reputation is strong enough to get you started.

## How do you get information?

You are being paid to find information for the customer that he or she cannot find. Successful newsletter owners never forget this important point. Your job is to search high and low for the best, most reliable information. You can get this information from industry magazines and newsletters, specialized libraries, a public reference library, books, associations, large companies, distributors' literature, executive speeches, television and radio, and from interviews with key people, personal observation, and personal contacts. Personal contacts are the people you respect in a particular field; call or visit them periodically to get a first-hand view of the field. Many newsletter owners start with great enthusiasm about a field, but after a few issues, neglect to pay close attention to personal contacts and information relevant to content.

You get your best information in the same way you become an expert in a particular field, by first-hand experience. For example, if you are doing a newsletter for veterans, and in a current issue you want to examine the quality of health care at the veterans' hospitals, you will need information from a number of sources. Talk to hospital administrators, doctors, nurses, patients, the families of patients, and other parties involved with health care. Get the complete story of veterans' hospital health care by reviewing all available information. Remember, there are two sides to all stories.

Do not generalize from research on a small part of the total subject area. If you have done research on only the local veterans' hospital in your area, Anyplace Bluffs, be careful not to generalize about national veterans' hospital care. For the sake of your credibility, gather information on several veterans' hospitals before you comment on national health care at veterans' hospitals. Newsletters need credibility to succeed.

Let's say, after interviewing and information gathering, you find that the hospital is doing a good job in delivering health care to the veterans in the Anyplace Bluffs area. Make it clear to your subscribers that this judgment is based on your examination of only one hospital. A reader living in another part of the country might otherwise conclude that all hospitals are fine, and act on this information. This reader would be upset on learning that his or her local veterans' hospital did not live up to expectations. The key point here is to avoid making a generalization based on limited information. You will be on safe ground when you say, "This report is on research from one veterans' hospital only; we will follow up this report with others that examine the national outlook on health care at veterans' hospitals."

# Be your own reporter

Reporting on research you have done is not as valuable as sharing your conversations with someone involved in your field or discipline. Ask a leader in a company or organization to give you an interview. Plan ahead by making a list of questions you would like to ask your guest. The following is an example of an interview.

> YOU: Thanks, Ms. Davis, for taking some of your valuable time for the interview.
>
> ANDREA: Please call me Andrea.
>
> YOU: Fine. Since you are President of the Board of Real Estate Professionals, what do you expect will be the average price for a single home this year?
>
> ANDREA: Around $134,000, this year.
>
> YOU: What income is necessary to purchase a single house?
>
> ANDREA: A household income of at least $50,000 per year.
>
> YOU: What can a buyer do to prepare for a mortgage?
>
> ANDREA: A buyer needs good credit and adequate income to become accepted by the bank. I recommend that the buyer also review his or her credit file.
>
> YOU: How do you get a review of your credit file?
>
> ANDREA: You can request a copy from your credit reporting agency. The credit reporting agency must send you your credit file if you're turned down for a loan.
>
> YOU: What common mistakes do most first-time real estate buyers make?
>
> ANDREA: They fail to take enough time before making an offer on their property.
>
> YOU: Thank you very much for the interview, Andrea.

The interview process is an excellent information-gathering process, and the beauty of this approach is that you get a chance to talk face to face. You can observe the facial movements and body language of the players in a discipline, field, or industry. Listen for hesitations and for intonations in your interviewee's answers. When your guest is located in a distant place, interview by phone. Each interviewer gives you more information and contacts. Use the interview process regularly.

# Check your facts

A lawyer reviews a case before going into the courtroom, gathering the facts necessary to present the best possible case for the client. Check out your facts *before* you publish the newsletter. Your readers are counting on you for the real facts, the story behind the story, and they will not accept a mistake from a respected authority, the owner of the publication. For example, if the unemployment rate in New York City is 8 percent and you said it was 18 percent, apologize in the next issue and never let it happen again. Readers of newspapers may accept mistakes because they understand the time pressures of its publication, but these same readers have no sympathy for incorrect information in a newsletter.

# Good content takes time

A successful newsletter is published on time. Give yourself sufficient time to put together a newsletter with content that will be a tribute to you. Don't wait until two days before the issue is due to write it. Time pressure will force you to accept lower quality than you would otherwise. We will discuss time management in more detail in Chapter 13 on marketing your newsletter business. I am the author of a recently published time-management book, *199 Time-Waster Situations and How to Avoid Them*. The book addresses common time-waster situations and solutions to deal with them successfully. Time is your most important resource—use it!

# Test your performance

How do you know when your newsletter is working, and becoming essential reading? Your most important test is the number of initial subscriptions or orders you are getting, but the most relevant area to *test regularly* is renewals. Your newsletter business has one important advantage over other businesses; you can test the percentage of returns from a mailing. For example, when you mail 1000 sales letters and receive 10 subscriptions, your percentage is 1. When you find a particular issue is a success, review it fully. What did it include to make it successful? Successful newsletters find the right formula, and continue to use it over and over.

Evaluate your newsletter each month. What is the strongest article or feature in that issue. Was the newsletter clear? Did it attempt to cover too much information? Did you communicate clearly and use space economically? Did your newsletter offer information that the reader could use immediately? Was the newsletter worth the $2.00 per issue cost? Did the newsletter give information on how an important subject will affect the customer? Put yourself in the reader's place. Examine your publication regularly. Testing will be discussed in much greater detail in Chapter 11 on marketing.

## Decision time is here

Now you need to decide on the content of your newsletter. In other words, what will you publish in your newsletter? Use a format such as the following to organize your content formula:

| | |
|---|---|
| _____ | Examples |
| _____ | Feature Articles |
| _____ | Graphs/Charts |
| _____ | New Product Section |
| _____ | _____ |
| _____ | _____ |

## Summary

Your content formula is the basic foundation of your newsletter. People judge your publication by it. By researching the specialized field of your newsletter and becoming an expert on it, your content, and your content evaluation will improve. You are both the editorial content manager and marketing manager. Keep testing to see what content approach is working. Hiring an expert to evaluate your data can be helpful. A successful content formula shows up in high renewals. Match your newsletter content with the needs and wants of your customers, and your own specific background and experience. Avoid generalizations. Become a subscriber to your newsletter by reading it carefully each issue. Be your own reporter, and visit your field of interest often. You decide on what products or services you mention in your publication. Just because you receive a sample product does not mean you are required to mention the product in your newsletter. Now let's write a winning newsletter!

# 5

# Writing winning articles

There is only one rule for successful writing: Write about a subject that you know well. Sounds simple, but too often a writer chooses an unfamiliar subject. The writing becomes choppy and hard to follow. The flow is lost, and so is the reader. Your writing must grasp your reader's interest and hold it throughout the journey through the newsletter.

Good newsletter writing style establishes rapport with your readers. You connect in a special way so that there is understanding and mutual respect. For example, a newsletter for a doll collectors' club discusses a Ginny as though the doll were real, and goes into great detail on the various dresses, dress patterns, and choices of designs for the outfits. The doll shows, auctions, sales, exhibits, and fairs are listed. A free pattern of doll tab overalls is enclosed in the issue. This newsletter owner has an excellent awareness of the interests of her market, and she writes in a refreshing manner.

## Plan your writing

You plan your trip to another state *before* you climb into your automobile. Successful writing also requires a plan, an understanding of the goal of your newsletter. It is important to review your choice of newsletter subject and name before selecting this goal. How will your target market gain from this newsletter issue? How compatible is this issue with your mission statement? How does it relate to the golden contract you signed with your prospective customers? How does this issue relate to the newsletter content you selected in Chapter 4? By carefully planning each issue, you establish your own quality control process. Planning prepares the way for your best writing.

## Use discipline

Discipline is part of good writing. Don't wait until you get into a creative mood. Write on a regular basis—during your lunch hour, before going to work in the morning, an hour or two before bedtime. By writing regularly, you can sharpen your writing skills, and you can prepare your newsletter drafts early enough to polish them for your readers. Discipline means keeping a file of notes and clippings, and reading in and outside your newsletter topic field. Discipline is locking the door in your study, office, or room until the job is completed.

Write an extra newsletter and keep it in a folder called "Emergency Newsletter," so that when a deadline is staring you in the face, and you come down with the flu, or some other emergency arises, you can put the next newsletter out on time. Although this is not possible for some newsletters, such as financial newsletters that depend on up-to-date information, others can publish a content that is not dated. Once you use up your extra newsletter, write another and return it to your folder. Like the spare tire in your car that is replaced once the original tire is fixed, replace your emergency newsletter when you use it.

## Use the storyboarding technique

Storyboarding, or brainstorming on writing topics, helps you expand and organize your ideas by using others as sounding boards for these ideas. I used this technique in a recent newsletter issue on company health benefits. I called a few people together to discuss these benefits. As the facilitator, I asked a simple question, "What should your company consider for health benefits?" As the ideas flowed, I wrote them down. I also asked, "What is the health benefit you would most like to see?" All members of my group were encouraged to contribute. No criticism was allowed. I encouraged members to build on the ideas of others. Figure 5-1 shows the results of this storyboarding ses-

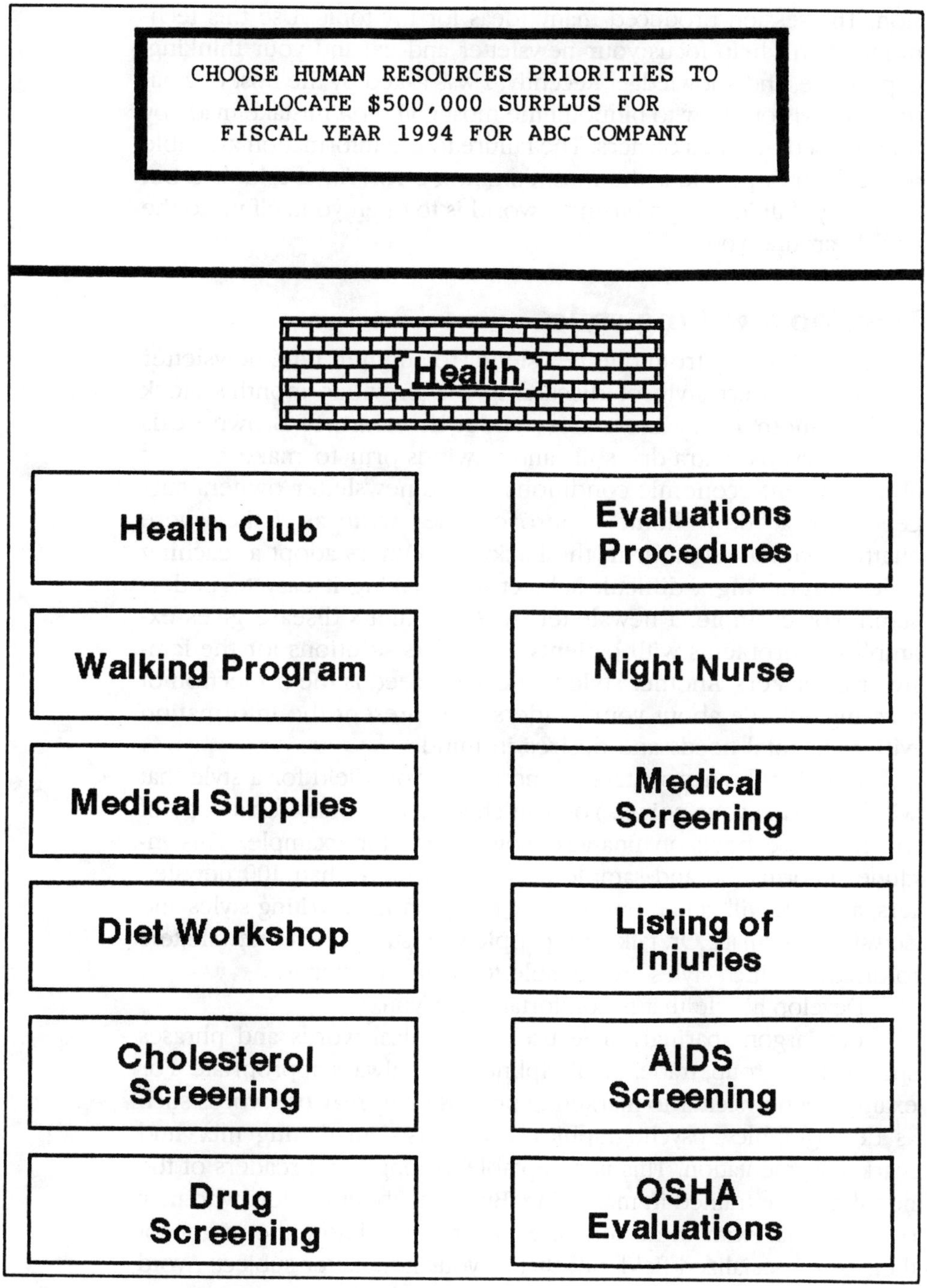

CHOOSE HUMAN RESOURCES PRIORITIES TO
ALLOCATE $500,000 SURPLUS FOR
FISCAL YEAR 1994 FOR ABC COMPANY

Health

| | |
|---|---|
| Health Club | Evaluations Procedures |
| Walking Program | Night Nurse |
| Medical Supplies | Medical Screening |
| Diet Workshop | Listing of Injuries |
| Cholesterol Screening | AIDS Screening |
| Drug Screening | OSHA Evaluations |

*Fig. 5-1. Results of storyboarding.*

sion. The session produced many ideas for my topic. Use this technique; it will help focus your newsletter and expand your thinking, experience, and knowledge. Recently, I was asked by the host of a national television show to pinpoint the most common mistake made by home-based business owners. The failure to use information available in the form of people is the most common error. An overlooked but necessary skill in today's business world is to open yourself up to the people around you.

## Develop a writing style

Writing styles vary from one newsletter to another. One newsletter may use a direct style of discussing the previous month's stock market. Another may use a story about how Farmer Brown deals with his crops, extra-dry soil, and a windstorm to make a point about current economic conditions. Some newsletter owners succeed with a "down-home" approach; they write as if they were chatting with a neighbor in the backyard. Others adopt a teaching style, introducing a difficult subject and making it easy to understand. For example, a newsletter on Alzheimer's disease gives examples of problems with patients and offers solutions for the family or caretakers. Another style that can succeed is the projection of a caring attitude about your readers; you present the information with their total needs and desires in mind.

Examine the newsletters in and out of your field for a style that will best make your points. You can check your library for a copy of the reference book on financial newsletters, for example. This includes information and sample pages from more than 100 newsletters, and you will get an opportunity to see various writing styles and newsletter formats. Or, talk with people who subscribe to newsletters to discover which styles are suitable for your newsletter.

Develop a style that is comfortable for you.

Use jargon sparingly. The use of technical words and phrases specific to a group, trade, or discipline is not always appropriate. For example, a newsletter to marketing professionals may use words such as demographics, psychographics, house lists, marketing mix, and market segmentation. This is acceptable as long as all readers of the newsletter are trained in marketing. But what about readers who may be unfamiliar with these terms? Some readers know the jargon of their own specialized field, not that of your newsletter subject. Avoid addressing your newsletter to a segment of your subscribers; present it to the majority.

Another element of writing style is the use of underlining to emphasize certain words in your newsletter. Kiplinger, which uses this technique, has become one of the most successful newsletters in the world. Be cautious about which words you underline; when you underline too many, the emphasis is lost.

## Do a first draft

Good writers do first drafts. Once your first draft is completed, let it rest. Put it down for an hour or two. (Some newsletter writers leave the first draft overnight.) Now pick it up and read it. Play the role of the reader. What can be left out? What can be added to help your reader understand? Are you overwriting? Newsletter readers expect a crisp, punchy style that moves along. What can you do to make your point clearer? What does each line have to do with the next one? Rereading and rewriting are essential. Start over again if you've lost the central message you want to communicate. Good writing results when you mold your first draft into a message the reader can see vividly. You will reach this special place in your writing craft by polishing your words and sentences so that they shine like diamonds.

Leave out the clutter in the way of the reader's understanding. Check the facts to be sure they are correct. Fix the misspellings and the little things you're not sure about. Small details left undone will cause a problem when time is critical, just before printing your newsletter.

## Get the reader's attention

Good newsletter writing gets the reader's attention. The same rule applies to writing advertisements, sales letters, and news releases, which we will discuss in Chapter 11.

Launching your newsletter requires getting your reader to sit up and take notice of your message. Examples of attention-getting messages, which are also called headlines, follow:

4 Credit Unions Closed in Rhode Island Today

Survey Shows Business Will Triple in the 1990s

Competing Successfully against the Japanese

Legislators Vote 25% Raise to Over $100,000 Annually

Income-Earning Real Estate Will Double in Value

Choose the most important feature of your issue and announce it in the first sentence of your newsletter. This will take your readers' attention away from ringing telephones, conversations in nearby offices, work to be done, and all other distractions.

## Maintain a good flow of information

Give your subscribers the information they need and want. The content of your newsletter is the reason they pay for your publication. Plan what you want to say and become an expert in your field so that you can write a convincing issue.

Good newsletter writing keeps moving along. Connecting one subject to another is one of the most important principles of writing newsletters.

A question I receive in my college seminars is: How many subjects for a newsletter issue are required to fill the body? It depends on the length of your newsletter; an eight-page newsletter requires more than the four- or two-page issue. I would rather have you prepare more subjects than too few.

Give your readers more information than they expect to receive. For example, let's say you're doing an issue on competing against the Japanese. You may want to include the following subjects:

Innovative quality controls

Quality control circles

Control charts

Brainstorming problem analysis

Upper control limits

Lower control limits

Profit-and-loss analysis

Profit improvement chart

Cost-benefit analysis

A new philosophy on quality control: Dr. Deming's contributions

Successful quality control

Choose the best material, and use it.

## Make your points clearly

Avoid being tricky or clever. Your subscribers want to fully understand your message. When your newsletter discusses a difficult point, for example, the cost of the savings and loan bankruptcy problems, show how this will affect the average person. How many dollars will the average person pay in taxes to correct the damages? Give examples of how some of your subscribers or associates are handling certain problems or opportunities. Nothing gets to the point better than a concrete example of someone dealing with a situation.

## Add visuals

People learn in various ways. You can tell someone about a subject, but if you show it, their understanding increases. When I write a word on the board, my students who learn visually enter into the flow of the class. In newsletter writing, a visual, such as a graph or chart, helps amplify or explain subjects.

The type of visuals you add will depend on your market and the difficulty of the material you are presenting. For example, the process flowchart in Figure 5-2 could be used for an issue on competing with the Japanese.

Visuals are also helpful when discussing the increase in the price of a stock during the last three years. Including a graph increases your reader's understanding. Review all opportunities to sharpen the body of your newsletter with illustrations.

## Close successfully

The best way to close is with energy and without wasting words. Some newsletter owners use the close as an opportunity to touch on an important subject, promising more on it in the next issue. This strategy gives the reader something to look forward to. A newsletter on executive skills uses the close as an opportunity to summarize key points of the issue. Other newsletter owners feel readers spend too much money for their publication for them to waste space on repeating key points; they feel that the subscriber can reread if necessary. Some newsletter owners sign with a positive thought to the reader.

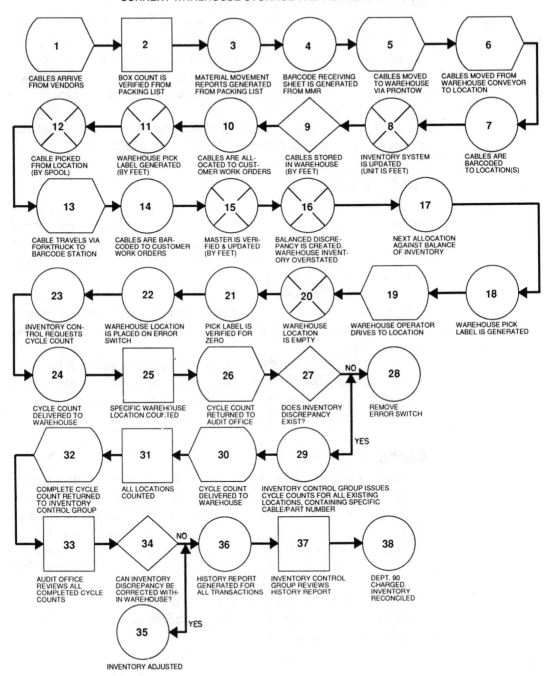

*Fig. 5-2. A process flowchart.*

Some newsletters use a signature at the close, while others do not. A signature from you makes the newsletter personal. It may be as simple as:

Respectfully,

Gary A. Smithurst
President of Model T
Ford Association, Mississippi

*or*

Cordially,

Rita A. Rolina
Publisher

Study various signature approaches. You make the final decision.

## Seek feedback and criticism

Good writers always look for new story ideas and comments both favorable and unfavorable on their newsletters. These might be in the form of a letter from a subscriber, a telephone call, or hearsay. When you have many comments on one area, consider taking action on it.

Some owners of newsletters solicit comments from their subscribers. For example, a newsletter owner on photography asks her readers to request articles they would like to see in the newsletter, and once a year she lets them vote on the best issue of the year and the reasons why they selected it. A personal thank-you letter is sent to each respondent. An owner of another newsletter on selling information checks his writing quality by calling subscribers after each issue is published to simply ask: "How did you like our February issue of *Selling Information Letter*?" He records their responses and thanks them for their time.

Like the restaurant owner who asks if you have enjoyed your meal when you are getting ready to leave, a newsletter owner who seeks feedback from subscribers ensures customer satisfaction.

## From beginner to master writer

Beginning writers, like beginning teachers, start slowly, use excessive preparation time, and stay close to their plan of action. As experience increases, the beginner writer moves away from a narrow focus to experience with more information, and also begins to use new techniques. For example, the beginning writer, like the beginner teacher, becomes a conversationalist, which is important in both teaching and writing. I taught with a wonderful man who wanted to motivate his students. His key interest was in helping them get into college. My colleague started a newsletter on the process of selecting a college or university. The newsletter is doing very well because my friend knows his subject, enjoys teaching, and has a special ability to explain complicated things so that others can understand. College grants, scholarships, foundation grants, and loans for students and parents are subjects in his successful newsletter. My friend uses the skills he already possesses to develop his newsletter into an exciting and growing publication.

How can a beginner writer turn into a newsletter writer? *Write every chance you get!* Write letters to your friends. Write often to family members.

One technique I used with success when I first started to write is writing letters to the editor of my local paper. You get a chance to see your name in print and a chance to read your letter over again. Start small, by writing a few sentences or a small paragraph on a subject you feel strongly about, or something you know well. The subject could be local schools, the death of a close friend, drug enforcement, gratitude to a teacher for an important contribution, starting a hobby, positive thinking, thanks to a member of your church for a successful Christmas party, uses for the old town hall, raising money for a student trip to Canada, or possibilities for retired people volunteering at the local library, hospital, or rest home. Share your knowledge, insight, experience, and feelings with others. In the process, you learn how to write. Writing is like learning to swim. You begin with the dog paddle, and you stay close to the low-level end of the pool. As you get stronger, you learn the side stroke and back stroke, and you move into more and more complicated strokes, which in turn improve your speed, coordination, and confidence. In writing, the more you write the more adept you become, and the easier it becomes to outline a particular subject in your mind.

Write the first draft of your letter to the editor, then go back and reread it. Is it clear? Did it make the point you wanted to make in the beginning? Cut back on the excess words, and add the necessary words; simply connect one word with the next. The key here is to *send* the letter to the editor. Most editors will edit your letter slightly, but in some cases there is no editing at all. Look for your letter in the newspaper. Read it over and enjoy it. You may even get a call from a neighbor or friend who read it. Enjoy the congratulations. You deserve it. Write your letters regularly. When you see yourself published, you begin to feel better about your writing. When you review something you wrote six months before with a new writing piece, you will see the improvement. Nothing succeeds like the feeling of accomplishment.

Article writing is another way to get experience and also exposure in a particular field. For example, a New England owner of a small management newsletter wrote and published a number of articles in accounting magazines before he started his own newsletter.

To get published in a magazine requires querying the editor as to whether the magazine would like an article on, for example, how to set up a set of accounting books for a small business. Sell your idea. Make certain a similar article did not appear recently in the magazine. The editor will then write back to inform you of an interest or lack of it. When there is interest, you write the article and send a copy of it to the editor. (Always keep a copy for your records; many things get lost in the mail or in processing at the publishing company.) You will get an answer within one or two months. When you get published, you not only have the prestige of publishing at a magazine in a specific field, but you can mention your newsletter in the byline of the magazine article, and include it with your sales letter to your potential customers. If your query or article gets turned down, just keep writing and submitting until your work is accepted.

## When you hire a writer

It is preferable for you to write your own copy, since you feel strongly about your topic and have drawn up both the mission statement and the golden contract. But, if for some reason you decide not to do the writing, you can hire someone else to do it. For example, a New Mexico newsletter owner who has targeted the bridal market collects all her ideas in a folder and goes over each one with the writer before the writing begins. They decide together what will be included in a particular issue. When the newsletter is completed, the writer is requested to mail an advance copy to the owner. The newsletter owner reads the newsletter right out of her mailbox, just like her subscribers. You can send yourself a copy of your newsletter even if you write it. Remember to take full responsibility for your newsletter content!

The more interest you show in your newsletter, the better the job the writer will do for you. You can pay a writer an hourly rate or a negotiated per-newsletter fee. A recent issue of a writer market book puts the cost of a two-to-four page newsletter at $200 to $400; the four-to-eight page rate is $500 to $1,000. Per-hour rates vary, but generally range from $20 to $60. These prices vary according to geographic location and the state of the economy. Don't sign any long-range contracts with your writer until you feel comfortable with the quality of his or her work and with your ability to judge the quality. Some newsletter owners give their writers a share of the profits as an incentive to high-quality writing. A 5 percent profit to your writer for each renewal is only $1.20 of a $24.00-per-year newsletter, and if the writer is good, you get to keep the customer for another year.

## Summary

Good writing, like good cooking, takes time and effort. Most importantly, write about something you know completely. Storyboarding helps build ideas, and planning is essential to success.

Good writing takes your readers on an enjoyable and informative journey because you know your subject and how to present it in a unique manner. Each successful issue gives you a chance to sell your newsletter to more people. Choose your own writing style. Concentrate on subjects you know very well rather than go off on tangents, which will upset your readership. Have respect for your readers and the willingness to go an extra mile to give them your best work. Understand that your best writing is the key to selling subscriptions and renewals. Write each newsletter as though it is your only issue.

Now it's time to do some editing.

# 6

# Editing your newsletter successfully

After your newsletter has been written, it should be edited for spelling and grammatical errors, sentence structure, clarity of expression, consistency, organization, and the like.

Editing does not take the place of good factual writing, but when the writer does sufficient research, rereads, and rewrites, editing will ensure a well-written newsletter. Like a coat of wax that makes a car shine, editing makes your writing look better.

## Hiring an editor

Someone other than the writer should edit the newsletter. If your budget does not allow for hiring an editor, ask a friend or family member to perform this function. If you—the newsletter owner—have hired a writer, perhaps you can act as the editor.

Should you decide to hire an editor, the hourly rate will be $12 to $40. Some editors are paid a flat rate of $60 per four-page issue. Rates vary according to location and qualifications of the editor.

Make certain your editor understands your philosophy, content, and target market, and reviews past issues of the newsletter. With an understanding of the past, the future can be addressed as a team.

## A teamwork approach

A Florida owner writes a newsletter on the empowered woman, and since her training is in sociology, the newsletter is filled with many references to sociology studies and statistics. The editor was hired to make the newsletter more readable and less technical so as to expand the readership. In this situation, there is a real need for the owner and editor to meet regularly to ensure that they are working in the same direction. Some of the questions posed are

What are the goals of the newsletter?

Are we getting the subscriptions with the present content?

Are we expecting too much from the editor, or the editing process?

What letters, comments, and evaluations have been received from readers?

What problems are likely to arise when the writer is technically oriented and the editor is trying to make the newsletter more general?

Communicate often, and keep all lines of communication open.

An editor can make the writer feel good about the newsletter manuscript while making the changes necessary to improve it. For example, I know one editor in Maine, who tells his writer, "I really enjoyed your issue on modern retailing, but you lost me when you talked about mall-site selection versus free-standing building selection. We need examples to satisfy our good readers." An editor grades, evaluates, and motivates the writer.

## Compiling a style sheet

A style sheet contains rules of capitalization, hyphenation, spelling, and the like. Consistency of style avoids confusion. An editor can compile such a style sheet for your newsletter. Or, perhaps the owner-writer will do so. For example, an Oregon owner of a newsletter on teaching children at home compiled her own style sheet after reviewing several examples and referring to the *Chicago Manual of Style*.

## Ensuring clarity

The clarity of the newsletter contents is evaluated by your subscribers at renewal time. Editing ensures that ideas are clearly presented. One instance of enhancing clarity is shown below.

> The government report was late to the committee.

> The *federal* government report was late to the committee.

The preceding paragraphs referred to both a federal and a state report. The insertion of the word *federal* eliminated ambiguity.

Editing can add variety by substitution of appropriate synonyms and can also improve the flow of your sentences.

## Monitoring copy flow

A newsletter owner from North Carolina, writing on quality in the workplace, focuses on a steady flow of information for each issue. Her newsletter editor, who is her nephew, edits the newsletter so that the central focus of this information shows through in every issue. Sometimes an editor finds that certain copy is not complete and suggests that it be expanded. Editing monitors your writing goals of getting the reader's attention, maintaining a good flow of information, making your points clearly, and closing successfully.

## Editing keeps readers friendly

Editing keeps your newsletter bias free. Some people are very sensitive to gender bias. You do not want to irritate any of your readers.

For example, one writer used the term *salesmen*; the editor changed it to *sales representatives*. Another writer wrote, "The spokesman for the organization is Rebecca Smith." The editor exchanged *spokesperson* for *spokesman*. A writer of a monthly newsletter on banking referred to all bank tellers as women.

Another writer submitted the following sentence: "When the engineer arrives, he is to report to the main office." The writer used the masculine pronoun when the gender of the noun was not revealed. The editor changed the sentence to read: "Upon arrival, your engineer is to go to the main office." Editors are sensitive to instances of bias. Editing removed a possible source of irritation to the readers.

## Giving the manuscript to the editor

It is important to make editorial changes while the newsletter is in manuscript. Corrections at a later stage of production cost time at a critical point in your schedule as well as money.

A New Jersey newsletter owner delays his writing until the last minute, and he regularly turns it over to his editor late, expecting the edited version back within hours or, at the latest, the next day. Is it any wonder that the editing and the newsletter are not of the highest quality? You cannot expect quality editing when you don't allow your editor sufficient time.

Double space your manuscripts so that interlinear changes can be clearly seen. Check for correct spelling, grammar, repeated information, inaccuracies, lack of flow, and departure from the chosen style so that your editor can focus on other issues.

## Summary

An editor adds an important dimension to your newsletter. It is helpful for the editor to know the field and have an understanding of your subscribers. Editing maintains a good copy flow. Teamwork between the writer-owner of the newsletter and the editor is essential. Editing improves the quality of the publication and leaves your readers looking forward to the next issue.

Now let's discuss proofreading.

# 7

# Proofreading
# with care

Now your newsletter issue is edited. I know you're anxious to get your "baby" out to all your friends, associates, and readers, to share your new service. But first the newsletter must be proofread.

## What is a proofreader?

A proofreader is someone who reads final copy, or proof, to detect errors. Your proofreader can smooth out the final rough edges to give your newsletter a winning image.

## Hiring a proofreader

A family member or a friend may have the skills and interest in this position. For example, a newsletter owner in Michigan asked her husband, a technical writer for an electronics company, to proofread her newsletter on small businesses. Or, if your newspaper has a classified section, you can advertise for a part-time proofreader. Rates for proofreaders are $7 to $12 per hour. Choose someone who can work within your time frame. There is nothing worse than discovering that your proofreader is in Europe when the proofs need to be read.

It is best not to have the writer or editor be the proofreader. Proofreading should be a separate function. The editor and writer look at the newsletter as a whole; the proofreader focuses on details. The editor and the writer are so involved with the content, style, and flow of information that minor mistakes may slip by.

The proofreader should talk with the editor to be certain they agree on the proofreader's duties and the deadlines.

## The proofreader's duties

You send your proofreader a copy of the proof and the edited manuscript before the issue goes to the printer. (You keep the original, just in case the proofreader's copy gets lost in the mail or the proofreader does not meet your deadline.) The proofreader will compare the final newsletter against the edited manuscript. The proofreader will do the following:

Check spelling

Recheck arithmetic in charts

Check telephone numbers

Check unusual or technical words

Check names of people in photographs

Check for sense

Check grammar

Look for broken type

Review spacing

Check that the style sheet has been followed

A proofreader will use marginal marks with corresponding indications in the copy to inform you, and ultimately your typist or typesetter, of the corrections. See Figure 7-1 for a list of proofreader's marks.

Sometimes, a proofreader is asked to attend to content as well. In this instance, the editor must keep the proofreader informed about innovations and changes in the field.

Some proofreaders double-check with another proofreader. Once your proofreader finishes with all the corrections, the proof may be turned over to someone else to be proofread again.

Sometimes a proofreader sees the corrected copy to make cer-

## PROOFREADER'S MARKS

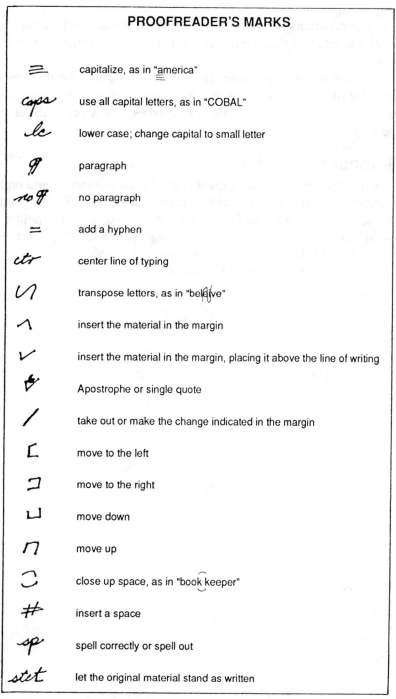

| | |
|---|---|
| ⹀ | capitalize, as in "america" |
| *caps* | use all capital letters, as in "COBAL" |
| *lc* | lower case; change capital to small letter |
| ¶ | paragraph |
| *no* ¶ | no paragraph |
| = | add a hyphen |
| *ctr* | center line of typing |
| ⸦⹋ | transpose letters, as in "beleive" |
| ⋀ | insert the material in the margin |
| ⋁ | insert the material in the margin, placing it above the line of writing |
| ⸕ | Apostrophe or single quote |
| / | take out or make the change indicated in the margin |
| ⊏ | move to the left |
| ⊐ | move to the right |
| ⊔ | move down |
| ⊓ | move up |
| ⊃ | close up space, as in "book keeper" |
| # | insert a space |
| *sp* | spell correctly or spell out |
| *stet* | let the original material stand as written |

Fig. 7-1. Proofreader's marks.

tain that no errors have been left in the new version. When the proofreader is satisfied that the proof is error-free, it is released to the editor.

In the finality, the owner has full responsibility for the newsletter. The owner should read the final proof before the issue goes to press. If the proofreader overlooks mistakes, a new proofreader must be found.

## Summary

Proofreading can save you a great deal of disappointment and embarrassment. When you read the first copy that comes off your printing press, you don't want to find that on page two, you misspelled the word *and* as *amd*. This is not the image you want to project. Save your image by having a 100 percent correct newsletter!

Now let's design your newsletter!

# 8

# Designing
# your newsletter

Newsletters have changed greatly since *The Boston News-Letter* was
published in 1774. With the many design options available today, it is
possible to achieve a unique, distinctive look for your newsletter. The
advent of desktop publishing, in particular, has made many innovative
options available to the owner of a home-based business.

What are these design options? Elements of design include the
following:

Text and display typefaces

Alignment of text type

Masthead

Logo

Color and weight of stock (paper)

Size and number of pages

Format (number of columns; indentation of paragraphs; spacing
on page)

Number of colors of ink

Line drawings

Photographs and other halftones

Self-mailer or insertion in envelope

Stapled single sheets or folded paper

Review the newsletters you have at home, or visit your local library. Ask yourself the following questions that relate to the newsletters' design:

What makes the newsletters look attractive?

Which ones are easy to read and understand?

What newsletters get your attention?

What elements in these newsletters stand out?

Is it the masthead, the logo, or the title and subheading that gets your attention?

Is it the headlines that get you attention?

Does the manner in which the newsletter connects one subject to another compel you?

Make a list of the elements most likely to complement your newsletter.

*First impressions count.* Choose a design that fits the topic of your newsletter. The design should enhance your newsletter content, whether the subject is business, consulting, or doll collecting. Each issue should be so attractive that the reader reads it to the end.

Decide on a design, and continue to use it. Nothing confuses a reader more than one newsletter issue with one format followed by another in a totally different format.

## The format

Like the concrete foundation that supports a building, your newsletter format supports your contents. First, decide how many pages will be in your newsletter and what the size of these pages will be. (For example, the most popular size for a four-page newsletter is 11 by 17 inches.) Then choose a format for these pages.

There are three basic formats: the single-column, the two-column, and the three-column format (see Figure 8-1). Some newsletter owners choose the single-column format simply because they use a

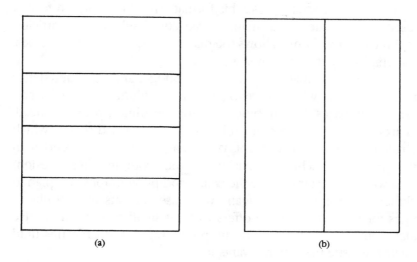

(a)                                    (b)

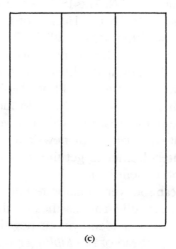

(c)

*Fig. 8-1. The basic newsletter formats:* (a) *one column,* (b) *two columns,*
(c) *three columns.*

typewriter or word processor, and can paste a copy of their masthead on the first page of the print-ready issue before sending it to the printer. The two-column format is often chosen when charts, graphs, and photographs are used. Many business, investment, hobby, health, and recreation newsletters use this format. The three-column format is used in newsletters that include a variety of subjects and articles. The three-column format allows the maximum space for long articles, photographs, charts, and other graphics.

Choose the format that will fit your budget and your newsletter topic. Experiment with one-, two-, and three-column formats by creating sample pages. Lay out blocks of type, headlines, your masthead, and art on sheets of paper or on board sheets. (Board sheets, which are ruled with the measurements of the page, can be purchased at an art supply store.) Which format works with your masthead design? Which will best accommodate the charts and photographs you plan to include? For example, a Michigan owner uses various sizes of photographs for the newsletter he offers to local small manufacturers. He experiments with placement of the photographs and drawings until he gets the issue the way he wants it.

## The masthead

The masthead is the top section of the first page of your newsletter in which you give the name and address of the newsletter, the editor's name, the issue number, and the ISSN.

A word here about the ISSN. The ISSN is the International Standard Serial Number assigned by the Library of Congress, 101 Independence Avenue, SE, Washington, DC 20540. Write to them for information about getting this number assigned to your newsletter. The value of this number is that newsletter buyers, researchers, and librarians can find your newsletter easier. It will be classified in a particular index. Don't wait until you get the ISSN to do the first issue of the newsletter. But add the number later. It will help you get exposure to your newsletter, and it will make your newsletter look more professional. Not all newsletters bother to get the ISSN number, but many successful ones do, and benefit by it.

Your masthead can be very elaborate, or it can be simple. Choose your masthead carefully. The masthead is the same, issue after issue, and will help the reader identify your newsletter.

For example, the masthead of *The Kiplinger Washington Newsletter*, one of the most successful newsletters ever published, uses a sim-

THE KIPLINGER WASHINGTON LETTER

*Circulated weekly to business clients since 1923—Vol. 68, No. 4*

THE KIPLINGER WASHINGTON EDITORS

1729 H St., N.W., Washington, D.C. 20006-3938 Tel: 202-887-6400

*Fig. 8-2. A simply designed masthead.*

CAREER PUBLISHING COMPANY 358 Main Street - Suite 20  Haverhill, Massachusetts 01830 (617) 374-8051

*Circulated to business clients monthly*                *Volume 3, No. 5*

*Fig. 8-3. A masthead using reverse-type artwork.*

ple rendition of the title, a statement of circulation, the letterhead in the center, and a small logo in the top left corner (see Figure 8-2).

The *New Career Ways Newsletter* uses reverse-type artwork (Figure 8-3) in their masthead. In reverse-type artwork, the ink is printed around the outline to show up the image. Reverse-type artwork is an eye-catching alternative.

## The logo

A logo is a graphic image representing an individual, company, or product. Your logo should give the reader insight into your business or field. Choose a logo that will reproduce easily. It should be used in all your issues as well as on your sales letters and brochures.

Some newsletter owners with graphic expertise and/or the inclination develop their own logos. But you may want to have your logo done by a graphic designer. A North Carolina newsletter owner recently stated, "I am so happy I turned over the logo assignment to a graphic artist. I spent many hours trying to design one, and the results were not very good." Before employing a graphic artist, ask for an estimate. You may want to get as many as four quotations before choosing a graphic artist. Remember to tell the artist approximately what you are willing to spend, so that you and the artist are in the same ball park.

## Typefaces

Letters, numbers, and symbols come in a variety of designs. Select the typefaces that will give your newsletter the most favorable appearance.

Type is either *serif,* which has "feet" at the edge of each letter, or *sans serif,* which is plain (see Figure 8-4). Many newsletters use serif type because the owners feel that readers can read it faster. Many newsletters use sans serif type for headlines or subheadings because it attracts the reader's eye. There are various designs for both serif and sans serif type. Choose a typeface and stay with it. Don't be like the New Jersey newsletter owner who got into the habit of using serif for one issue and sans serif for the next. Her readers became confused because the newsletter lost visual consistency.

Type size must be large enough to be read easily. Usually, 10- to 14-point type is used. Once you choose a type size, continue with it. Don't change the size of the type to accommodate more copy. Cut nonessential copy when your newsletter is too long. Or, save an article or item for another issue.

| | |
|---|---|
| It's not easy growing up with perfect hair. While all the other kids were out having split ends or getting bad perms, I was always home alone trying to downplay my golden highlights. The taunts were cruel: "Hey, Vidal Sassoon!" or "Is that your hair or are you wearing a helmet?" Hey, I may not have frizzies, but I do have feel- | It's not easy growing up with perfect hair. While all the other kids were out having split ends or getting bad perms, I was always home alone trying to downplay my golden high-lights. The taunts were cruel: "Hey, Vidal Sassoon!" or "Is that your hair or are you wearing a helmet?" Hey, I may not |
| (a) | (b) |

*Fig. 8-4.* (a) *Serif and* (b) *sans serif typefaces.*

## Type alignment

Type alignment is another element of design. The example below is of flush left type, ragged right, which simply means that only the first letters in each line of type are aligned.

> We will see you then.
> The article starts out by
> explaining that utilities

The informal ragged right affords visual variety on the right margin and offers few or no hyphenated words. Some readers feel that ragged right text adds to the speed of reading.

Another alignment possibility is justified type, in which the last letters as well as the first are aligned. Justified alignment usually incorporates hyphenated words. The *Supervisor's Bulletin* (Figure 8-5) uses justified type. Review the flush left and right alignment example below.

> The car ran over the card-
> board box in the driveway.
> The box split, and the con-

There are other design options for your type presentation. For example, *The Kiplinger Washington Letter* (Figure 2-3), which uses the flush-left ragged-right alignment, emphasizes the first few words in each paragraph by underlining and indenting them about five spaces. Notice also that the paragraphs are short.

## Art

Graphs, line drawings, and photographs can enrich your newsletter. Remember to use captions on your artwork. Captions are one of the most-read sections of a newsletter. Make certain you put the correct information in the captions. Captions can be placed above, on the side, or beneath the artwork.

Many new newsletter owners overdo graphic effects. Photographs, charts, and illustrations are costly, both in time and dollars, and using too many may detract from your newsletter flow. Many newsletters succeed with a simple typewritten page design.

## Graphic devices

One way to get your readers' attention is a strong headline. A New Jersey newsletter owner targets professional writers, new writers,

JUNE 30, 1987
NUMBER 760

## IN THIS ISSUE:

## SUPERVISOR AND EMPLOYEE:
## Who Is Working for Whom?

**What is your function as a supervisor? To be in command of a group of people who do work for you? To be the boss? Before you answer these questions, ask yourself another: "In the final analysis, just who is working for whom?" When you think about it, you should come to the conclusion that you are working for your employees, says this manufacturing manager.**

"Your function as a supervisor is to provide service for your employees," states Leon Sujata, Manufacturing Manager, Subassemblies and Factor Support Group for **Avco Lycoming**, a division of Textron, Inc. (Stratford, CT). "Your job is to get roadblocks out of their way so they can do their work and constantly improve their skills."

After all, how well subordinates do in their jobs is the yardstick by which management measures *your* performance. So any steps you take to assist workers to get their jobs done actually helps you get your job done.

Of course, that doesn't mean you should think of yourself as subordinate to your workers, Sujata says. But you should make sure that your attitude is geared toward assisting them, rather than expecting them to assist you.

### Helping Workers Do Their Jobs

It's clear that you have a stake in doing everything possible to help subordinates do their

*Fig. 8-5. Use of justified type in a newsletter.*

agents, editors, and artists. She uses headlines that reflect the theme of the issue to get her readers' attention. Good headlines set the tone for the issue, and ideally should be short, clear, and bold. Figure 8-6 shows different headline designs.

Another newsletter owner uses photographs to form the borders of her newsletter (see Figure 8-7). Still another device is to use pull quotes, which summarize key points, in your margins (see Figure 8-8). Pull quotes attract the reader to articles and are useful to readers who simply skim the newsletter. Magazines use pull quotes successfully.

## Desktop publishing

Desktop publishing has changed the way newsletters can be produced. Now, the home-based business can create print-ready copy on a computer system. Desktop publishing software has special features to help you with formatting, display type, typesetting, graphics, illustrations, and printing. Take a day or two to investigate various software packages. You will learn how to move sentences and paragraphs

*Fig. 8-6. Different designs for headlines.*

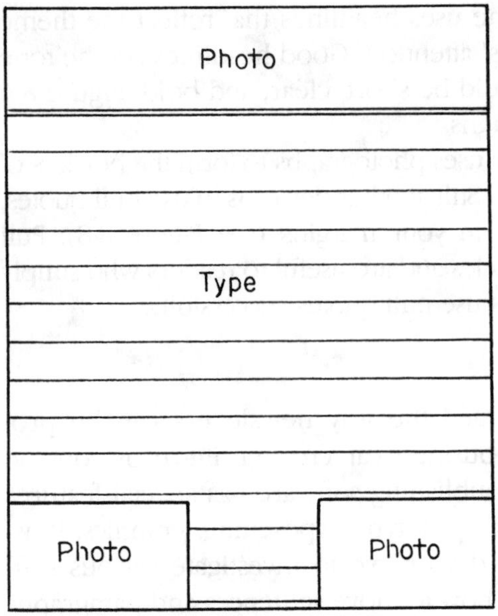

Fig. 8-7. Use of type and
artwork to form borders
in a newsletter.

**A ski area has
agreed to scale
down development
plans and to
continue to assess
the effect of its
expansion on the
black bear
population.**

Fig. 8-8. An illustration of the use
of pull quotes.

from one part of the text to another, how to add and delete words without having to alter the rest of the copy, and how to create a professional look with bar charts, illustrations, and graphic techniques. Choose the package that fits your needs.

## Summary

Good design is important to your success. Choose a masthead, logo, and format. Decide on those design elements that best express the content of your newsletter. The first impression your subscribers will have of your newsletter will be visual. Choose a design and stick with it. Your readers will come to identify your publication by its design.

Now let's discuss printing the newsletter.

# 9

# Printing
# your newsletter

Now you are ready to print the first issue of your newsletter. You must choose a printer and provide that printer with the pages of the issue in layout form. The printer will use these camera-ready pages to produce your newsletter. You must also decide how many copies of the issue to print, and buy the paper to print it on.

Some newsletter owners want to cut corners by photocopying their first issue. This practice is not advisable. Photocopies are not as good as printed ones. Your subscribers will be able to tell the difference. Don't jeopardize your image as a professional doing professional work. Don't compromise your research, writing, and editing to save a few dollars.

## How many copies should you print?

In the beginning you lack subscribers, but I still recommend that you print 1000 copies of your newsletter. You will want to save copies of your first few issues; you might want to include copies with your sales letters to increase your subscription list. Sometimes extra copies are sold at a future time as reprints. For example, let's say you devote one issue of your newsletter to getting financial aid and grants from the United States government. You can promote *Grants and Aid Free from the United States Government* in your current sales letter on reprints, and when your business grows, in your publications catalog. Some reprint buyers might even turn into subscribers.

## Choosing a printer

Printers vary in the quality of their work and the services offered. Some offer two-color printing, which means black and one other color—blue, red, or green. Others do four-color printing. Some can handle many different jobs, from business cards to complicated books. Others restrict their services to printing sales letters, brochures, and newsletters.

At least one month before you expect to print your newsletter, visit or telephone some printers in your neighborhood. Tell the printers about yourself, your goals, your newsletter, and the date you will need the printed issue each month or week. Impress on the printers that you are looking for a long-term printing relationship. Printers like the idea that they can depend on steady work and will price your job accordingly. Be specific. Ask the printer how many days, for example, it will take to produce a 1000-copy four-page newsletter on 1 sheet of 11 by 14 inch paper, folded in half.

Compare prices but look for quality. Get as many as five different quotes from printing shops in your area. (You might get a better price in Overtown Bluffs, but it takes more than two hours to drive there and back. Save your precious energy and drive for the creative writing and research techniques for your subscribers.) Ask to see some of their latest printing jobs, especially other newsletters they print. Does their work look professional? Is the printing clear? Does it have extra ink spots, smudges, or tears in the paper?

Ask to see a choice of papers. Notice the thickness, or weight, and the finish of the papers. You might want to use a different color than white for your newsletter. Some newsletter owners use a gold or an offwhite color to give their newsletters a different image. Once you choose a paper, you should continue to use it, so choose carefully. Make sure your printer has enough of your paper to keep the paper uniform, issue after issue.

There are two types of newsletter owners when it comes time to print and buy paper for their newsletter. Type A newsletter owner simply looks over the samples and selects. Type B newsletter owner spends excessive time with the printer, reviews extra samples, checks all the grades of paper, chooses a color for the newsletter and then changes it, decides to buy the paper in bulk to save money and then decides not to. Too much time and effort is spent with the printing of the newsletter.

Printing decisions can improve with experience. Avoid buying paper in bulk until you have had a few newsletter issues printed. Storing the paper and bringing it to the printer for each issue is time-consuming.

## Evaluate the printing job before paying for it

Take plenty of time to review the printing job before you take out your checkbook to pay for it. Answer the following questions before you pay for the work.

Is it the right color ink?

Is it the right color paper?

Is there overprinting or underprinting?

Are there smudges on the finished job?

Was the correct number of issues printed?

Did the printer deliver on the date promised?

Does the invoice agree with the quotation from the printer?

Pay only for the charges included in the quotation.

## Laying out your first issue

You have chosen a printer. Your articles and other copy are written, edited, proofread, and put into type. Your artwork is captioned and camera ready. You have a logo and a masthead, and you have chosen a format and other elements of graphic design. A copy of your sample pages is at hand. You are now ready to lay out the camera-ready copy of your first issue. Use board sheets or plain sheets of paper that correspond to your sample pages to lay out your newsletter issue. (See Figure 9-1.)

Doing a layout is like arranging furniture in an apartment. Where do you place your couch? Bed? Table? Bookcase? Television? VCR? Which items of furniture can be discarded? Which items should be

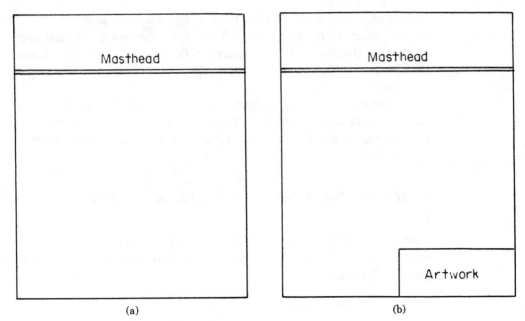

(a)                                                        (b)

*Fig. 9-1. Two sample newsletter layouts.*

put into storage? Your goal will be to use the space in your newsletter to the maximum.

Strive for quality, and not just quantity, speed, and convenience. George, a successful owner from New Mexico, provides a quality newsletter, mails it out on time, and gives excellent service. One key element in this owner's success is keeping the newsletter simple to assemble, by limiting artwork and design elements.

Set up priorities for each item in your newsletter. The article on food poisoning, the feature on the credit squeeze, and the article on the deepening recession must be included. Place priorities also on the art that accompanies each article. Place your most important items first, and then fill in with less essential content.

Don't try to rush the process. Review your issue to see that it fulfills your mission statement, that a theme holds it together, that it is easy to read, and that it is attractive to the eye.

Make certain to deliver your camera-ready copy to the printer in time for the issue to be printed on time. Ask your printer how many days in advance of your deadline the camera-ready copy should be delivered.

## Summary

Printing quality is important to your success. Like the restaurant down the street, which succeeds because of the high quality of its food and its attractive decor, your business will be judged by the quality of your content and of your printing, from your first newsletter, to your business card, to your sales letter, brochure, and order card. Your subscribers will judge you on everything they see and read about you and your business, so make certain that printing quality adds to your successful image. Compare prices, but never overlook quality. Give the printer enough time to do a good job. Choose your paper, and continue with it regularly.

Prepare your layouts carefully, taking care that the issue is visually attractive as well as well balanced in content. Get your camera-ready content to the printer in ample time.

Now let's turn to mailing your newsletter!

# 10

# Mailing your newsletter and direct mail promotions

You can plan, research, write, and produce a top-quality publication, but unless you use a workable, economical mailing system your newsletter will never be successful. You will be using the mails for both sending your newsletter to subscribers and for direct mail promotions (see Chapter 11). Sometimes a newsletter owner will piggyback a sales piece, such as a renewal letter, to their newsletter.

Watch the weight of all mailings. Invest in a small postal scale and weigh all mail so that you can monitor cost and avoid return of mail.

## Your first mailings

I recommend that you handle the addressing and mailing of your first newsletters and direct mail promotions yourself, so that you can learn what is involved.

When sending your newsletters, make certain that you get the names and addresses correct. Give your subscribers personal service.

One way to make the image of your newsletter top notch is to add any titles of the subscriber to the name and address. Remember to complete the ZIP code, and for your own sake and for the subscriber's, add the expiration date to the address. Please review the name and address of a subscriber below:

Dr. William J. Smithurst
167 Melrose Avenue
Haverhill, MA 01830-2048

By addressing William J. Smithurst as Doctor, and others as Professor or Reverend, you are showing respect for the person. You want to work to earn customer trust by giving a quality publication, and superb customer relations. It is satisfying to send your first issue to subscribers, or to friends and potential customers. Address your newsletters correctly and clearly.

At first, use first-class mail for newsletters. Other methods of delivery will be slower. Don't risk upsetting time-conscious subscribers. If a large number of your subscribers live in the same general geographic area, investigate sending your newsletters by presorted first-class mail, which is less expensive.

*Addressing Systems.* After your newsletter has been in operation for a while you will want to do mailings to potential subscribers each month when you send out your newsletters. You may want to invest in an addressing system to save you time and money. Many personal computers are being sold with a database program, so you can address your newsletters alphabetically, by region, by ZIP code, or by town. Some database systems have renewal dates, enabling users to send renewal information to subscribers in a piggyback mailing.

A good addressing system can help you build up your list so that you can do a variety of mailings, and someday start a second newsletter or rent your list to a noncompeting business or publication.

Charge more for foreign subscriptions. You just received one subscription from Ireland, and another from France. Once your excitement abates, you are faced with sending these newsletters by air mail. Charge at least $10 more for foreign subscriptions. Make certain that the price for foreign subscribers is listed on your order card.

Use third-class bulk rate for direct mail promotions. Presorted third-class bulk rate is half the cost of first-class mail, but delivery is slower.

You can apply for a bulk-rate permit at the post office. Bulk rate is for a minimum of 200 identical pieces of mail of equal weight. The mailer must presort the mail by ZIP code; SCF zone, such as 018 in the ZIP code 01830; state; and geographical zones. When you have eight or more pieces in one classification, put an elastic band around them and label the pile accordingly. The banded and labeled piles are put into a box, which is usually supplied free by the post office, and brought to the post office for weighing, checking the sorting, and payment. If the sorting is not done correctly, expect the post office to insist on your doing it correctly. The bulk rate should be used only for nontimely material, such as direct mail promotions. *Never send newsletters or invoices by bulk rate.*

Delivery time for third-class mail depends on where the mail is sent. If you live in California, your California and Nevada mail may arrive in a few days; your mail to Chicago may take a week; the mail to New York and Massachusetts may take a week and one half to two weeks. Delivery time depends on the total volume of mail at a given time, the volume at the local post office in, for example, New York, and the clarity of the addresses. Many factors can delay third-class bulk mail.

## When your business has grown

At a later stage of your business ask for a second-class mail classification for your newsletter mailings. Most newsletters qualify for second-class mail rates, which are delivered almost as quickly as first-class mail for about half the cost. You must apply for the special rate at your local post office. To qualify, you must presort the mailing and recipients must pay for the subscriptions.

When your newsletter has 1000 or more subscribers, and you are sending more mailings to potential customers, you might consider hiring a *letter shop.* The letter shop can send out your newsletters, address a direct mail promotion to your mailing list, and even insert your sales letter, brochure, and order card into envelopes. The letter shop can do one specific job or a complete mailing from start to finish, permitting you to concentrate on other areas of your business.

## Use the services of the post office

The post office offers seminars periodically, and also sells books on the regulations and techniques of the postal service. The postal service answer line has made it simple for people to find out about hours, locations, rates and classes, international mail, mail order fraud and security, and the like. See Figure 10-1 for an example of postal answer line services. Your post office is very important to your success in the newsletter business.

## Summary

Mail the first few issues of your newsletter and your first direct mail promotions yourself. Send your newsletter by first-class mail and your direct mail promotions by third-class mail. See if your newsletter qualifies for a second-class mail status. When your subscription list has grown, use a letter shop for all your mailing needs.

Now let's discuss marketing your newsletter!

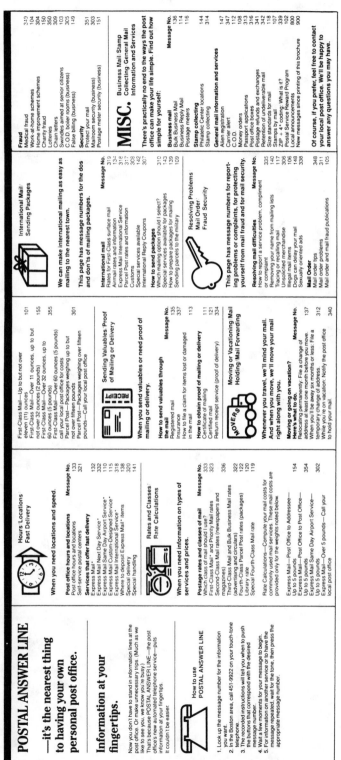

*Fig. 10-1. U.S. Postal Service "Postal Answer Line" instructions.*

# 11

# Marketing your newsletter creatively

Now that you have mailed out your first issue of your newsletter, it is time to focus on your marketing program so that you can build your subscriber list. Your goal is to make some money. You can earn money by making your newsletter profitable. And some newsletter owners also earn money from consulting opportunities developed from marketing their newsletter.

In my introductory college course, I define marketing as the numerous activities that direct the product or service from the producer to the consumer. Marketing is the bridge that permits your newsletter to move from the producer, in this case you, to the consumer, the subscriber of your newsletter. The foundation of this bridge includes selling, advertising, pricing, and public relations. Selling, advertising, and pricing are discussed in this chapter. Public relations is the subject of Chapter 12. Each plays an important role in your success.

## Is marketing an art or science?

Marketing is both an art and a science. It is an art because advertising and selling require creativity, awareness, and insight. It is a science because it includes research, planning, discipline, and analysis. Your chief job will be to review the selling benefits your first newsletter issue offers the readers and potential subscribers. Look at the mission statement and golden contract you completed in Chapter 3. Review your editorial calendar for the coming year. Review the reasons you decided on that particular newsletter subject. Go over your target market and its demographics and psychographics (data which give information on how people spend their leisure time). The more you know about your market, and what it wants, the better are your chances to sell to it.

## Do your own marketing

Some newsletter owners hire others to do their marketing, instead of doing it themselves. I don't recommend the practice. It is costly both in dollars and in loss of experience. The closer you get to prospects, the more feedback you will receive as to whether they like your newsletter, what they would like to see included in it, and other important input.

Take the example of an energetic, determined unemployed woman who developed a soda in her kitchen. She knew it had the potential to be the basis of a successful business. She had no money to hire an expensive marketing manager or consultant, so she distributed the product herself. She could not negotiate favorable contracts with distributors because she didn't understand the product herself. The gutsy woman wanted to succeed; therefore, she delivered bottles of her soda to the stores from the back of her jeep. Her budget was so small that she could only park her jeep at a meter with time remaining on it from the previous parker. She learned a great deal by selling her product herself; it forced her to understand how the process of marketing works. She learned about marketing by living it. She became the marketing research manager by hearing first hand, not from expensive surveys, what the customer wanted in the product. This home-based business grew into a multimillion-dollar business because the owner understood the product and the market. The owner recently sold her business to a billion-dollar national beverage company.

You too can learn about the market for your business. It means taking the time and effort to learn what makes the buyer purchase your product, what moves the prospect from the mental (thinking about) stage to the action stage of buying. Successful newsletter owners not only put out a quality newsletter with excellent content and good design that is geared toward their market, but they are willing to sell the newsletter as well. Nothing happens in the newsletter business until orders begin to come in. You need orders to spread the news to others about how your newsletter fulfills the market need.

## Pricing your newsletter

Pricing your newsletter is tricky because you must consider a number of important factors before you put the price tag on your service. Review the price for other newsletters in your field. Consider whether the competition is a weekly, monthly, bi-monthly (every two months), quarterly (every three months), or semi-annual (twice a year) publication. Consider the content you expect to deliver to your readers versus the content they receive from others. What special services do you perform for your subscribers? Some financial newsletters, for example, have hotlines, which means that subscribers can call the newsletter owner or editor and get their questions answered.

The basis of price is, of course, costs. The conservative, cost-conscious home-based newsletter owner might understate costs by looking at just the cost of printing. Let's say that your 1000 copies of a four-page newsletter cost $120 at the local quick printing company. Without fully examining the real expenses involved, you might estimate too low a price. Based on just the cost of printing and postage, the above example would yield

| | |
|---|---|
| $0.12 | Printing cost per newsletter |
| 0.29 | Postage per newsletter |
| 0.03 | Envelope per newsletter |
| $0.44 | Total cost each newsletter × 12 months = $5.28 per subscriber |

This cost estimate is misleading because it includes only a small amount of the expenses of your business. It fails to include the cost of writing and printing the sales letter, order card, reply envelope, and outside envelope for the sales package; the cost of your magazine advertising program; the cost of insurance, legal, and accounting services; the cost of supplies, word processor, filing, taxes, and telephone.

Let us say that your monthly telephone bill is $100 and that you have 1000 subscribers. Your telephone cost for one year is:

$$\$100 \times 12 = \$1200$$

Divide this by the number of subscribers to get the telephone cost per subscriber for one year.

$$\$1200 \div 1000 = \$1.20$$

Now divide this number by the number of months in a year:

$$\$1.20 \div 12 = \$0.10$$

Your telephone cost per subscriber for your monthly newsletter is $0.10. Once you determine the cost per subscriber per issue for each expense item, you will be in a much better position to price your newsletter.

Although there are other services that you can sell to increase your revenue, such as running seminars, renting your list, and selling books, you don't want these other activities to support your newsletter. You want your newsletter to be profitable.

Use the format below to calculate your expenses.

\_\_\_\_ Printing costs per newsletter

\_\_\_\_ Postage per newsletter

\_\_\_\_ Envelope per newsletter

\_\_\_\_ Telephone cost per newsletter

\_\_\_\_ Insurance cost per newsletter

\_\_\_\_ Office supplies costs per newsletter

\_\_\_\_ Taxes per newsletter

\_\_\_\_ Legal and professional fees per newsletter

\_\_\_\_ Accounting fees per newsletter

\_\_\_\_ Freelance writer fees per newsletter

\_\_\_\_ Marketing costs per newsletter

Notice how the price per issue is much higher than the original $0.44 once you take the time to review all your costs. Avoid pricing your newsletter until you understand all the costs involved. You don't want to have to increase your price because you're losing money. Get a good price and hold it.

*Maximum-profits pricing* results from reviewing the newsletter completely, taking stock of its image in the field, and setting goals to get a good share of that market. The maximum profits method of pricing looks at what the market can bear. Maximum profits result from a price low enough to look attractive to the market, and high enough to cover the expenses with a healthy profit. Remember that profit is the difference between total revenue (subscriptions) and business expenses. Profits result from a quality newsletter that continues to grow in subscriptions month after month, primarily by word-of-mouth advertising, from people interested in and enjoying your newsletter.

Choose a price that is low enough for your market, but high enough for you to make a profit and continue to publish. Look at both the gross revenue and your costs. Review the possible gross revenues below:

| Subscriptions | Subscription amount | Gross revenues, $ |
| --- | --- | --- |
| 1000 | $24 | 24,000 |
| 1000 | 36 | 36,000 |
| 2000 | 39 | 78,000 |
| 2500 | 49 | 122,500 |

Your price must attract the greatest possible number of subscribers. The lower the cost, the more customers will try your publication. Your job in marketing will be to convince your prospects that you have something of value to offer. Consider what the competition is charging for a newsletter similar to yours. When you charge a price similar or lower than the competition's and your quality is higher, your chance of increasing your share of the market is enhanced.

The *cost-plus pricing method* is most commonly used by newsletter owners. The price is determined by taking a percentage for profits above the cost of the newsletter and the overhead. The cost of the newsletter is primarily the cost of writing, editing, and proofing and of printing, postage, and artwork. The overhead includes the telephone, supplies, insurance, legal and accounting fees, and marketing and advertising costs. Many newsletter owners who use the cost-plus method continue to offer special incentives to make it easy for the customer to try their publication. (One example of a special incentive is a free three-issue trial subscription. Another incentive is a new article or pamphlet on traveling in Europe in the twenty-first century that will accompany your new subscription.) Once you settle on a pricing strategy, hold it until you get a chance to see how the public will respond to it. Avoid changing prices on your publication. Readers might feel that you're unsure of the quality and worth of your publication.

## Direct mail promotions

One way to attract new subscribers is with direct mail promotions. These include your sales letter, order card, and brochure and the envelope that contains them. Sometimes you may piggyback some of your literature to the newsletter itself. Other times you may send a separate package.

## The sales letter

In your business, revenue is essential. Without revenue, the business will fail. Sales are needed to increase the revenue, and in your business you cannot afford to send free copies of your newsletter to potential customers and friends in the hope of their eventually subscribing. You must sell virtually every day. Now that your first issue is printed you can send your newsletter along with a sales letter and order card. A sales letter is a very important tool in selling and marketing your publication because it presents an overview of the publication and its benefits to the subscribers. The sales letter is not simply words on paper, but a carefully planned writing piece that gets *Attention*, *Interest*, *Desire*, and *Action*. This process is commonly called the AIDA sales process.

*Attention* is attained by a good headline, something that includes more than striking the fancy of the target market; it should stop them in their tracks. For example, each target market has expectations of itself. Students want good grades, sales people want sales and commissions, consultants want clients, business owners want to earn money, pet owners want ideas on getting closer to their pets, sports fans want information about their teams, and financial investors want information on how to make their money grow.

First impressions count. In your sales letter you can use some of the following headlines to get those important orders:

How to Make Your Investment Grow in the Next 10 Years

Home-Based Businesses Are Growing and Thriving

An Exciting Newsletter on Nuclear Energy with a 10-day Trial Subscription

How to Develop Powerful Writing Skills Quickly and Easily

How to Travel in America on $50 a Day

How to Develop Relationships That Last, Grow, and Endure

Since the reader confronts hundreds, even thousands, of advertisements during an average day, a creative headline is needed to attract a consumer. Creative headlines are sometimes the result of looking at the newsletter in a different way. Step back and look at the potential reader and the newsletter together, and ask what important benefits of the newsletter will attract the reader. An important headline might be the reason why you started your newsletter in the first place. It might be in your mission statement. Use the space below to write down some headlines that will get the maximum attention from your sales letter.

1. _____

2. _____

3. _____

4. _____

5. _____

6. _____

7. _____

Go over the headlines. Put the less-focused ones aside. Work with the headline that will add spark to your sales letter. Try two different headlines, and chart the results to see which one pulls the most orders. For example, using headline 1 send out 1000 sales letters, and using headline 2 send out 1000 sales letters, and check your results for future use. Getting the right headline is essential to success.

*Interest* requires a steady flow of news about your newsletter. Explain why your newsletter is better than others in the field. What information, features, special interviews, forecasts, and analyses will be available in your newsletter? Will your newsletter be a summary of other business articles in the field? How can you offer unusual depth and comprehensiveness? Show the readers that you know their situations and their need for information. You care about them and want to share your information with them. In this part of your sales letter, try to establish a relationship with your reader.

*Desire* is the next step in the sales process, and this calls for more information about newsletter features in the months ahead. For example, typical subjects from a newsletter on speaking include:

5 Ways to Breathe Properly and Relax

The Basic Principles of Speech Organization

Planning Your Speech Strategy

How to Improve Your Beginning and Ending

Choosing Your Delivery Style

8 Most Important Principles to Make Your Speech Successful

Instilling desire in the reader is further developed by proving that the newsletter is received by other subscribers. One way to do this is to list testimonials from other subscribers. A testimonial is when people report their satisfaction about your newsletter. A sample testimonial is shown below.

> "The material is especially designed for me. It is worth your subscription price and more. It keeps me up to date with other real estate businesses in the country. Renew my newsletter for another year."
>
> JAMES HAGGERTY
> *Broker*
> *JH Realty*
> *Massachusetts*

A newsletter owner from Tennessee elicited testimonials by sending out questionnaires and by attaching response cards to renewal letters, urging his subscribers to fill them out. You can use testimonials in your sales letter once you receive the writer's permission. Permission can be obtained simply by writing a letter to ask for it. Use real customers, not family, friends, or associates; your customers are depending on your sincerity. Don't fall into the trap of rewarding people who offer testimonials by giving them free subscriptions. Once you pay for testimonials, you compromise their value, and you will lose in the long run. Be aboveboard and don't pay for testimonials. You will find that a testimonial will increase the effectiveness of your sales letter.

Desire is further developed by offering a guarantee to the buyer. A guarantee assures the potential buyer that you have confidence in your newsletter. Offer to refund the subscription price, with no questions asked, if the buyer is unhappy. Potential buyers will be more inclined to order when they know that they can get a refund if the publication fails to fulfill their needs. The guarantee is essential in selling today's consumer.

*Action* simply means asking for the order. Ask for the order now, right this minute. If the letter is put away, the order will never be sent out. Tell your prospect to fill out the order card, check the order card, mark the 12-, 24-, 36-, or 48-month subscription on the order card. Many newsletter owners give a free gift or a trial subscription if the reader takes a subscription. The gift is usually a special report on investments, the best career of the twenty-first century, how to improve your health or wealth, or how to invest in the next century. People are more apt to buy when they get a gift. Offer trial subscriptions carefully. When they're too long, readers tend to continue the trial until the end, and then cancel out.

A sales letter with all the elements of AIDA increases your chances of getting your share of subscriptions. See Figure 11-1 for a sample of a winning sales letter. Writing a winning sales letter is difficult. The average return for a sales letter sent out using the direct mail method is ½ to 1 percent of the total mailed. When you mail out 1000 letters at 1 percent return, you can expect to receive 10 subscriptions, and if you mail 10,000, you will receive 100 orders. Once you get a winning sales letter, do not change it in any way until you find sales beginning to drop. Do not loan your sales letter to another newsletter owner or others selling related services. You might find your sales letter competing with similar sales letters. Once you get a winner, keep it to yourself. Bite your lip before you share your success with others, or you will find many competitors at your door.

## The order card

The last sentence or paragraph of your sales letter should tell the reader to immediately fill out the order card. The order card, or reply card, summarizes the offer you are trying to make to the reader. Many

# NEW CAREER WAYS
## NEWSLETTER

NEW CAREER WAYS • 2 Margin St. • P.O. Box 822 • Salem. Mass. 01970          Editor: William J. Bond

*Circulated to business clients monthly...*

How To Put Your Business Career
INTO HIGHER GEAR

Whether you feel your career is on a plateau, or if you
believe things are going well, but could be even better, I'm
certain your plans for the future could get some new thrust
from NEW CAREER WAYS, as explained below.

As a busy executive, you simply don't have the time to spend
sifting through the many business publications there are
available to sort out the career-building information you
need to know.  But NEW CAREER WAYS can do it for you.

My staff does hours of digging to accumulate meaningful
information, which forms the basis for wide-ranging reports
that you can put to practical business use.  And their articles also include descriptions of how managers and business-
men in different states are handling the same issue or
problem — for a many-sided view of the situation.

But despite such unusual depth and comprehensiveness, NEW
CAREER WAYS is brief and fast-moving.  It's not filled with
advertisements and articles of little or no interest like
business magazines.  In the shortest possible time, its concise
yet meaty articles give you the extra thrust you need to mesh
your skills, talents and knowledge into a highly profitable
and satisfying business career.  For only $2 a month - $24 a
year - you can't afford to be without NEW CAREER WAYS.

For instance, here are a few typical subjects from forth-
coming issues:

        How you can cut your business expenses.
        How you can do more in less time.
        The success secrets of the million dollar salesman
        How to get the raise you deserve.
        How you can successfully handle people.
        How to write better letters, memos, reports and analyses.
        What future job opportunities will be made available
        to you.
        How you can do your own career planning.

And besides these far-reaching reports, you'll receive other
valuable information - encompassing such areas as the latest

*Fig. 11-1. A sample sales letter.*

business books, new business techniques and trends, government
regulations, practical business strategies, new ways to sell
yourself to your subordinates and customers.  Because NEW
CAREER WAYS is a total career-building package.

"The material is exciting, informative, and enjoyable. I stop everything when NEW CAREER WAYS Newsletter
comes -- it makes my day.  Keep up the better work."

Frank B. Schroeder
Travelers Insurance Company
Danvers, Massachusetts

"NEW CAREER WAYS Newsletter is filled with new ideas
to help me move ahead in my career.  Your subjects
are fascinating, written in a concise, to-the-point
manner.  Keep up your excellent newsletter."

J. Doherty, Manager
Lynnford Company
Lynn, Massachusetts

"Your newsletter appears to me to be extremely
valuable.  After 13 years of editing (Academic)
business journals, I have concluded that newsletters
are the way to reach managers.  Practicing managers
don't read academic magazines; the few that do, don't
find precepts in them.  I wish you well."

William G. Ryan, Executive Editor
Business Horizons Magazine
Graduate School of Business
Indiana University
Bloomington, Indiana

And here's what business magazines are saying about NEW CAREER
WAYS:

"... an unusually perceptive and down-to-earth newsletter especially designed to help the junior executive operate and manage his or her career successfully."

THE NATIONAL PUBLIC ACCOUNTANT

"... an excellent way to keep up to date on new
business techniques... and helpful to you in moving
ahead in your business or career."

THE FLORIDA BUSINESS DIGEST

*Fig. 11-1. (Continued)*

marketing consultants and experts agree that the offer, which is crucial in the success of the proposal, includes the newsletter, terms, price, guarantees, and how to complete the order card. The order card essentially ties up all points mentioned in the sales letter. The order card should be a separate piece of paper. Often readers will not take the time to cut an order card that is attached to a sales letter. See Figure 11-2 for an example of an order card.

How long will it take to get an order from a direct mail promotion? It may take a week for the first order to arrive, but you will continue to receive orders for the next two weeks. The amount of orders you receive will depend on the quality of your sales letter and your list, and the attractiveness of your offer.

Keep testing what is working in your offer by examining each order card. For example, if you get an order for one year's subscription to your newsletter, with a request for the free booklet on *Traveling in New England*, make a note of this on your customer's file. The order card can also tell you how the customer heard about you. For example, let's say you placed a classified advertisement for your travel newsletter in the *California Travel* magazine, and you sent them your order card to complete the sale. In order to key, or trace the source

---

## Check and return this form promptly

### NEW CAREER WAYS
### P.O.Box 822 ● 2 Margin St. ● Salem, Mass. 01970

Circulated to business clients monthly...

YES, sign me up for NEW CAREER WAYS Newsletter at the special charter rate of $2.00 a month payable annually. (This special offer includes the exciting executive report "Minding Your Own Time" FREE)

Send us_____ additional copies at $8 per year each for distribution to our supervisory personnel (all to same location).

☐ Bill Company          ☐ Bill Me          ☐ Check enclosed

Company_____

Name_____Title _____

Address_____

City_____ State_____Zip_____

Make check payable to NEW CAREER WAYS

REFUND GUARANTEE: The unused portion of your payment will be returned to you on **request at any time.**

---

*Fig. 11-2. A sample order card.*

of, the order, write CTM–1CA on the back of your order card. CTM–1CA stands for *California Travel* magazine–January classified advertisement, and you can note this in your sales records. By using the keying system you can determine where your customers are hearing about you—from your list, other newsletters, classified advertisements, or personal contacts. Continue to use the methods that are working, and review the ones that are not.

## The brochure

Another important element in your marketing strategy is the brochure, which can be included in your direct mail package. A brochure is a selling piece that can include some selling benefits, motives, and advantages not listed in your sales letter. (See figure 11-3.) The brochure is another way to view the newsletter and its editorial objectives and advantages. Some newsletter owners use the brochure to discuss the qualifications of the writer of the newsletter, or the training and qualifications of the editor or research staff. The brochure can be used to inform readers that they can expect concise, worthwhile reports.

## The outside envelope

The outside envelope contains your sales letter, order card, and brochure. The outside envelope must be opened or you will never sell the potential customer. Some newsletter owners write a message, the *teaser copy,* on the outside envelope to induce the reader to open and read the contents. (See Figure 11-4, showing an outside envelope with a teaser copy on the bottom front.) Once the contents are read, the AIDA process can operate to sell your newsletter. Some messages you might use on your envelope are shown below:

> A Special Publication to Help You Earn More Money
>
> How to Choose the Best Career of the 21st Century
>
> How to Buy a House with 5% Down
>
> Investments with the Smallest Risks
>
> Fundamental Human Resources in the 21st Century
>
> Information Inside on 199 Time-Waster Situations
>
> How to Get a Raise in Pay Tomorrow
>
> How Successful Women Manage
>
> Managing Stress and Opportunities Successfully

*About the editor...*

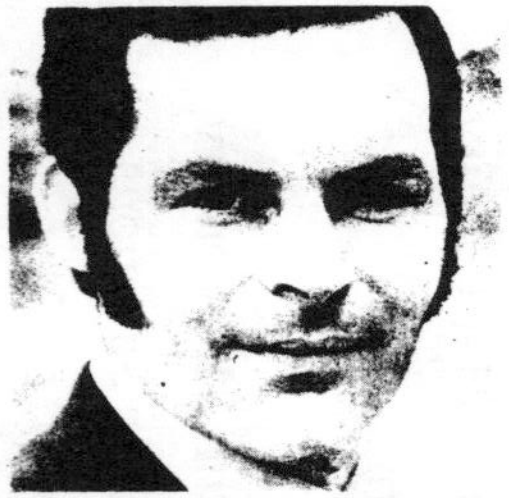

WILLIAM J., BOND editor of NEW CAREER WAYS is Assistant Treasurer of North Shore Recycled Fibers Corp., Salem, Mass. He holds a Master of Arts degree from Salem State College, where he received his BS degree in 1968. Mr. Bond has written widely in professional journals, most recently in THE NATIONAL PUBLIC ACCOUNTANT, TEXAS CPA, THE AMERICAN CHAMBER OF COMMERCE and EXECUTIVE JOURNAL. He has written a book, and is presently working on a second book. Another article will appear soon in THE PRIVATE CARRIER MAGAZINE. Mr. Bond resides in Haverhill, Mass.

NEW CAREER WAYS has a full commitment to your career and business success.

Each edition of NEW CAREER WAYS is designed with your career advancement and business profits in mind.

Make an investment which will grow and develop – subscribe to NEW CAREER WAYS today. Simply fill out the enclosed postpaid postcard and mail to:

NEW CAREER WAYS
P. O. Box 822
Salem, Massachusetts 01970

NEW CAREER WAYS NEWSLETTER

"The unique way to come out on top in your career and business."

***Office • Sales • Technical • Supervisory • Executive***

*Fig. 11-3. A sample brochure.*

Historical Roots Newsletter
67 Melrose Ave.
Haverhill, MA 01830

A NEWSLETTER TRACING YOUR PAST TODAY

*Fig. 11-4. An outside envelope.*

The best message may be in the mission statement you developed in Chapter 3; it could be in the golden contract you planned, or in the customer bill of rights, or in the newsletter content strategy you so carefully constructed.

## Ask for the subscription

Many new subscriptions are gained by the newsletter owner following up the sales letter and order card with a phone call. Your newsletter subscription sale might need the little push of calling and asking for the order. Remind the customer that your publication has many benefits, ideas, techniques, principles, which are not discussed in other publications, and that therefore it is in his or her best interest to buy a subscription from you today. Do your own telemarketing. Review your mission statement just before you pick up the phone to call the potential customers, and ask for their support. Your telephone is a good selling tool.

*Put your telephone number on all your communications.* People want to call you to ask about your subscription rates, your policy on cancellations, your subject area, your content philosophy, and some might just want to discuss a subject in your newsletter. Make yourself available to others by including your telephone number on your newsletter, your sales letter, order card, and brochure. This will add credibility to you and your newsletter. If your phone is unattended during the day, put in an answering machine. The public has become willing to talk to an answering machine. People reason that it's far better to leave a message than to hang up after the answering machine has picked up on the call, thereby avoiding the expense of a wasted phone call. Answer all your calls. You will find that many telephone calls turn into subscription sales when you show genuine interest in the caller, and ask for the order.

## Responses to mailings

Expect a return of from 1 to 1½ percent of your total mailing. If you send 1000 direct mail packages, and you get a return of 1½ percent, you will receive 15 subscriptions. If you charge $39 per subscription, your sales for that mailing will be $585. Remember that there are costs involved in each mailing. Review the profit and loss below to determine if the 15 subscriptions will make a profit for you.

### Profit/Loss Newsletter Mailing
#### January 1, 1998

| | | |
|---|---|---|
| Sales (15 subscriptions) | | $585 |
| Less costs: | | |
| Renting mailing list | $ 50 | |
| Postage and mailing | 150 | |
| Printing of sales material | 165 | |
| Total expenses | | 365 |
| Profit in mailing | | $220 |

What do you do with the profit? Invest the $220 profit in a small-space advertisement in a national magazine (discussed later in this chapter), and with the names of the people who respond to your advertisement, sell subscriptions and build your prospect list.

## Hitting the target market

Now that you have decided on what strategies you will use in your sales material, you must decide what vehicle you will use to reach the target market. One of the best methods is to rent a mailing list of the prime customers for your newsletter. Notice I said *rent.* Companies, associations, and people rent their lists; they do not give them away or sell them. When you rent a mailing list, you can use the names for one time only; you cannot copy the names and addresses. You can retain a name and address only if the customer buys your newsletter subscription, or writes back to you, or contacts you in some way. Then the name and address becomes your property. One of the most popular questions in my newsletter seminars is how the list owner can keep the people who rent their lists from making a copy. The list owner salts the lists, which simply means including names in the lists and monitoring the mail sent to these names. If the list is being used illegally, they will be aware of it. Once they determine which people are using the names illegally, they will stop renting to them. Since lists are always being updated, you want to maintain good relations with list owners.

A carefully chosen mailing list can direct your mailing package—your sales letter, brochure, and order card—to your potential customers. The most popular mailing list rented by newsletter owners is the mail-response mailing list. The mail response list is rented through a list broker, a person engaged in the business of bringing people and lists together.

Here are some possible mail-response mailing lists:

Small Business Bookbuyers

Law Journal Subscribers

Consumer Economics Newsletter Expires

Newly Trained Bookkeepers

Personal Computer Owners

Spreadsheet Software Buyers

New Charge Card Holders

Writers' Magazine Subscribers

Photography Newsletter Expires

Florida Fruit Mail Order Buyers

Sports Car Buyers

Correspondence School Students in Automotive Repair

Buyers of Micro Workstations

Health Food Buyers

Children's Book and Record Buyers

Inspirational Video Buyers

Buyers of Computer Supplies

Mailing list brokers can be found in the yellow pages of your phone book. You should give the broker a copy of your newsletter, and your direct mail promotion. Ask the list broker to recommend the best three or four lists for your newsletter. Choose the list that best meets your target market demographics and psychographics. Ask the following questions before you spend $75 or more for each 1000 names rented from the list broker:

Who is on this list?

What is the age group?

What is the income level?

When did they last buy by mail?

Do they buy newsletters and books?

Where do they live?

Do they belong to a certain professional group?

Are they members of an association?

Ask your list broker for a breakdown of the proposed list, according to demographics and psychographics. Go further and ask the list broker for the names of people who rented this mailing list in the past. Call or write these people because they can give you valuable information about their results. A good mailing list must be accurate. Some list owners will give you extra names or a small refund when you receive returnables, that is, mailings that are returned to you because peoples' addresses have changed. A mailing list is only as good as the accuracy of its names and addresses.

*Conduct a test mailing first.* Many newsletter owners plunge right in and rent a lot of names before they know whether the list will work for them. Don't fall into this trap. Ask your list broker for the minimum rental order for the "Restaurant List" for your newsletter on customer relations and restaurant management. The minimum rental might be 3000 or 5000 names. Order the 3000 minimum order, for example, and ask that you get the national mail sort, which means that your mailing list will be a national cross section. There will be people on the list from Maine to California, and it will be representative of the whole list. By doing a test mailing, you can review your results before you rent more names. Let's say your rental list has a total of 100,000 names. Rather than renting 10,000 or 20,000 of these names before you know the results, test the 3000 minimum. Make your list broker work for you.

Another list many newsletter owners use is *the compiled list,* which you can compile yourself from directories, trade show lists, sales records, leasing records, and business listings in magazines, newspaper articles, and even city and town directories. Some newsletter owners creatively use compiled lists. For example, George compiles a listing of new boat buyers and sends them information on how to subscribe to his boating newsletter. A list can be compiled by using the directories and listings available at your local or regional library. Once you compile your own list, it is your property. When you find your compiled list is working, keep using it until it stops working.

*The house list is your wealth.* The house list is the names and addresses of the people who subscribe to your newsletter. Once on your house list, you can keep selling them month after month, year after year. In the beginning of your business, you never loan this list or give copies of this list to anyone. You must build this list up over the following year or two. The people on this list are special to you because they responded to your offer, and even with intense competition, they continue to purchase from you. This is your own list, and ideally it should comprise only buyers. Inquiries, the people who write to you and ask for information or a sample copy but don't buy, are not buyers and do not belong on your house list. Review your house list often. What changes are taking place in your house list? Are there more people from the South, the West coast, the East? Are you getting more orders from doctors and dentists than from veterinarians? Are you getting more orders from businesses than from individuals? Are you getting more association members ordering your newsletter than individuals? Check your house list often, and look carefully at any changes. Once your business is well under way, you might consider renting your mailing list to other businesses for extra revenue.

Learn which lists are working. Key your order cards to determine which lists bring in the business. Let's say that you are using a list of attorneys from a law magazine, and on the back of your reply card you can use a key—AT—to signify the attorney list. Keep a good record of sales from each list, so that you can make future decisions on list rentals with solid information. Good marketing means good record keeping and good data.

What about renting a mailing list from another related newsletter? This is an excellent idea. Check with your mailing list broker to see whether or not any related newsletter owners or business magazine owners are renting their lists. Some newsletter owners will only rent out their expires, or inactive, list, which is of subscribers who decided not to renew their subscriptions. In your marketing program, keep trying to get your expires to reconsider and return to your newsletter. Never quit on former customers! The expires list is important, almost as important as your house list, and it should be reworked hard before you give it up.

## Advertisements

A newsletter owner on energy runs small-space advertisements and classified advertisements in *Popular Mechanics*. Run your advertisements in magazines that have many advertisements. See Figure 11-5 for an example of space advertising. Obviously, advertisements in these magazines bring in business. Some newsletter owners offer a free copy of the newsletter to specific markets, just to get them to read their newsletter. Here is a potential classified advertisement:

> Free newsletter on energy sources for 1990s. Write to: Energy Newsletter, 10P Main Street, Freetown, MA 00018.

Once you receive the order, look for the key 10P, which shows you that the response was the result of your advertisement in *Popular Mechanics*. When you send out a follow-up sales letter and reply card soliciting a subscription, put the code 10P on the back of your reply card to show that this order would be the result of the advertisement in *Popular Mechanics*.

To further test your sales material, and if you are using two types of sales letters, A and B, on the back of the reply card write the key

# Historical Roots Newsletter

*By noted historian and lecturer*

*William J. Bond*

*25 years experience*
*tracing lineage to ancient times*

**Historical Roots Newsletter features**

**guidelines for the lineage process**

**how to use birth, marriage, death certificates**

**checking previous research**

**passenger lists**

**cemetery headstones**

**name changes**

**birth certificates**

**deeds**

**and**

**military records**

*Write today, request FREE Sample Copy*
*Historical Roots Newsletter*
*67 Melrose Ave.*
*Haverhill, MA 01830*
*508-372-7957*

*Fig. 11-5. Space advertising.*

10P-A to signify that it was obtained by an advertisement in *Popular Mechanics* followed up by sales letter A. Good newsletter marketeers keep a close check on what sales material and what advertisements are working to get the orders.

A recent advertisement in a consumer magazine offered a free three-issue subscription to a financial consumer newsletter. The advertisement stressed "Send me three free issues. No obligation." and also gave a special discount to customers who wanted to continue the newsletter. Your advertisements should stress the reasons why your publication is different and why the customer should at least take it on a trial basis.

The key to successful small-space advertisements is consistency. Keep advertising, month after month. Give your advertisement a chance to work. Too often, a newsletter owner will try one advertisement in a magazine, get a few inquiries and only one or two subscriptions, and then quit in disgust. Keep running those small-space advertisements or classified advertisements because eventually they will pay off for you by building your subscriptions and prospect list.

The best magazine to advertise in is the one that has a good subscriber base for your newsletter. If your target market is engineers, advertise in an engineering magazine that reaches this market. If your target market is writers, advertise in the two writers' magazines, *The Writer Magazine* and *Writer's Digest,* in order to reach the bulk of the writers in America. Refer to Chapter 2 of this book, when you analyzed your target market and determined that your competition was in two or three magazines. You might find that a small advertisement in these magazines can open the door to many subscriptions, providing your sales material is strong enough to sell your newsletter.

Write to various magazines and ask for their rate cards. The rate card will give you information on the amount of paid circulation, that is, people paying for the magazine rather than getting it free. Readers are not necessarily subscribers. They may be people who get a chance to read the magazines from the coffee table in a waiting room at the dentist's office, or at the lounge at work. Such readers are called *pass-along circulation.* The total readers might be two or three times the total circulation. For example, if the circulation of the magazine is 100,000, the readers could swell to 200,000. The readers may respond to your advertising program, but your best response will be from the paid subscribers, the people who paid for the magazine out of their hard-earned income.

Choose the magazine that offers the best group of people who can benefit from your newsletter and are willing to pay for it. Choose a magazine that offers subscribers who have the income to buy products and services. Be willing to run your advertisement on a regular basis to give the magazine readers a chance to ask for and review your newsletter offer. Your classified or small-space advertisement is an excellent way to keep your product or service in front of your prime market all year long. Keep a record of your advertisements similar to the one below:

| Date | Magazine | Type adv. | Number of replies | Amt. of sales, $ | Cost of adv. $ | Profit, $ |
|------|----------|-----------|-------------------|------------------|----------------|-----------|
| Jan. 2000 | *Popular Mechanics* | Classified | 100 | 590 | 89 | 502 |

One newsletter owner in Harrisburg, Pennsylvania, makes an advertising profit analysis for every advertisement. Each advertisement she runs must either break even or earn more sales than the cost of running it. Continue to advertise every month for the whole year. Your market will continue to examine your offer all year long, so make it available to them.

*Follow up your advertisement with your direct mail package!* Once Sandra Jones, a subscriber to *Women's* magazine where you ran your classified advertisement, writes to you for more information, immediately send her your sales letter, brochure, and order card. Each inquiry can become a potential subscriber, and can go on your list of prospects. Some newsletter owners send out two or three direct mailings to try to convert the inquiry into a subscriber. Small-space advertisements are an excellent opportunity to get to meet your market by examining all inquiries.

## Use many marketing methods together

Some newsletter owners run successful small-space advertisements, and on a regular basis send out direct mail promotions to a designated list, or to their list of prospects to keep the sales going. Marketing is a never-ending process, from talking to people on the phone about your newsletter, to discussing the newsletter with a local business group, to getting new sources of customers from the magazine or newspaper in your field, to sending a thank-you note to a recent subscriber, to sending out a special offer to make it easy to buy a subscription from you. One newsletter owner ran a successful marketing campaign by offering a rebate. When a new customer purchased at least one full year's subscription, a check for $5 was sent to that customer. A national, prestigious newsletter company offers many extra gifts, such as special reports on the world's economy into the next decade, on how to manage businesses, and on the cost of health care. You have some ideas on how you can improve your publication offer. Good marketing shows the potential customer the value of the newsletter and how this value will more than pay for the small cost of the newsletter. Continue to test which free reports, booklets, or manuals will pull the most orders for you.

## Selling is everything in your business

And everything you do in your business is selling, from getting your sales letter written and printed, to coming up with sales promotion ideas such as rebates or a new advertisement, to the way you talk to people on the phone. Your potential customers and subscribers want to be sold, with a good product, but also from a newsletter owner with confidence and a sense of urgency in selling the best newsletter publication in the country or the world. When you're excited about your business, it comes across in everything you do, and people will respond positively to you. The keys to success are a quality product and a marketing plan that works hard for you.

## What will be the marketing costs for the first year?

Between $500 and $1000 for the first year. Some of this marketing money can come from the subscriptions you sell during the first year. In order to get orders, you need a good sales letter, brochure, and an order card; these are the essential tools to your marketing success. The sales letter is your salesperson, to tell your story to others; the brochure gives more details about the newsletter and you; and the order card is essential to get the information about the subscriber for the order. Small-space advertising in magazines that communicate to your target market is an inexpensive technique to keep you and your publication in the view of the market all year long. Some new newsletter owners want to rent lists and do heavy direct mail, which means heavy printing costs. I recommend that in the first year you concentrate on sales material to be sent in response to inquiries and on small-space advertisements; hold off on list rental and direct mail promotion until later. During the first year you should concentrate on building your house and prospect lists. Here is just an estimate on your realistic marketing costs for the first year.

| | |
|---|---:|
| 2000 sales letters printed | $175 |
| 2000 brochures (one-sided) | 80 |
| 2000 order cards | 50 |
| 2000 envelopes | 100 |
| Small-space magazine advertisement | 300 |
| Classified advertisement in related magazine | 280 |
| Total | $985 |

This estimate is low, and is designed to simply get you started on little more than a shoestring, but it includes the basics. When the subscriptions start to come in, you can increase those advertisements that are working, and print more sales materials. I just received a call from one of my seminar attendees, the owner of a sales management newsletter, who made the mistake of printing up too many copies of a sales letter before testing its effectiveness. Printing 2000–3000 sales letters gives you a chance to test the copy, to see if it communicates directly to the potential buyer. The one real benefit to your newsletter business is that everything can be tested, from the advertisement you run in the magazine to the sample copy of your newsletter enclosed with your sales letter. Did the direct mail packages with the free sample copy pull more orders than the package without the sample copy? Good marketing is taking action, then testing, and then taking action again. Now let's set up a marketing plan.

## Your marketing mix

The marketing mix is your strategy for your product pricing, promotion, and distribution. The product mix is your own view of your product, how you would like your product to be seen by your potential customers, and how it will become part of your marketing mix. One newsletter owner commented on his product mix by stating "*My* newsletter is the best publication on business law for small business in the country." Use the space below to write out your own product strategy.

_____

_____

_____

_____

_____

The pricing strategy is the final price you will charge for your newsletter. The pricing strategy considers fully the value you offer in your newsletter tempered carefully with what the competition is offering the market. Some newsletter owners price their newsletter lower than other newsletters and also offer a special introductory price to make the publication more attractive to the potential customer. Use the space below to fill in your pricing strategy.

_____

_____

_____

_____

_____

The promotion strategy includes how you will advertise your newsletter, whether it will be small-space advertisements in excellent mail-order magazines, classified advertisements, display advertisements, or direct mail to reach your target market. Your promotion strategy might also include a combination of both the small-space advertisements and direct mail to your prospect list, or rental of outside lists to reach your target market. Try to select a strategy that is different from the promotion strategies used by other newsletters. Many newsletter owners would like to promote their newsletters with radio and television advertising, but the prices of these media are very expensive. It would be best to wait until your business is firmly established before considering advertising in these media. Choose a promotion strategy that features such ideas as trial subscriptions, rebates, and discounts. Use the space provided to write out your promotion strategy.

_____

_____

_____

_____

_____

   The final strategy is the distribution strategy, which helps you to get your product into the hands of your potential customers or target market. Other owners will be happy to tell their subscribers about noncompeting newsletters that they feel their customers would enjoy. Many orders can be obtained by this method. A Michigan newsletter owner used her compiled list to sign up new subscribers. Another owner used associations to help him get his newsletter sold. Use the space below to write out your distribution strategy.

_____

_____

_____

_____

_____

   These market strategies will serve as your summary statement. Keep working on your summary statement, and have other people read it over to make sure that they fully understand it. Marketing is communication, and it will be up to you to communicate your marketing strategies to both your customers and your associates and employees on a regular basis.

## Summary

Marketing is the bridge connecting your newsletter to the customer. Marketing includes pricing, selling, and advertising. Get involved in the marketing yourself. Pricing your newsletter requires knowing your competition and your costs. Review the maximum-profits pricing and cost-plus pricing approaches. Your direct mail, a sales letter, order card, brochure, business card, and envelope with teaser copy are all marketing tools. Use the telephone to ask for subscriptions. Hit the target market directly. Mailing lists include mail-response lists, compiled lists, and your own prospect list. Small-space or classified advertisements can increase your revenue and build your prospect list. Choose the best possible magazines to use in your marketing program. Check each advertisement to determine whether it was profitable or not. Follow up the advertisement inquiry with your direct mail promotion. Use many marketing methods together.

Marketing can only be successful when you keep the marketing or selling focus in everything you do. Everyone is involved in marketing. Marketing is everything. Marketing must be practiced in all areas of your business from sending out a sales letter to thanking a customer for a newsletter subscription, from writing a thank-you letter to a newsletter owner for giving your newsletter exposure, to handling a customer complaint. All are marketing in action. Your newsletter and your newsletter business develop a reputation, and in order for them to establish a good reputation, a marketing focus on customer satisfaction is required.

Now let's discuss another part of marketing, the public relations activities that are so important in your newsletter business.

# 12

# Powerful public relations techniques

When you watch television and see a guest on the business talk program, that guest was selected because of public relations. The guest talks about the U.S. economy and discusses investment opportunities for the next two to five years. Calls are taken over the phone from callers all over the country, and as the show ends, the host informs the viewers that the guest is the founder and owner of *The Small Business Investment Letter* based in Denver, Colorado. This exposure can be worth thousands, perhaps tens of thousands of dollars in promotions to your business, and it costs not one penny.

When you read your favorite magazine, and a newsletter owner is featured in a full-page article, public relations influenced the magazine writer to choose the subject. When you turn the dial on your radio in the car, or at home, and listen to a guest talking about her new book, article, product, achievement, or newsy item, you can bet that her appearance was because of public relations. This chapter considers many public relations ideas. Use them to get valuable exposure for your newsletter.

# What is public relations?

Public relations is a marketing tool that is concerned with the public image of your newsletter. Good public relations informs the public of what products and services your company owns and sells, including the important reasons why they should buy from you.

Public relations is important because it is *free*—yes, *free*. Many of my seminar attendees find this hard to believe, but it is true. Public relations is using publicity to inform others about your newsletter, about the introduction of your new newsletter, or about a special article or item in your newsletter. Publicity is the art and the creative manner you use to get the media to carry a news story, or a newsy item about you or your publication. It matters little whether the story is about you, or your newsletter. It is important only to communicate to the public and people within your field of interest.

# The news release

Publicity uses the news release as the main tool. The news release has the following characteristics: (1) It is a summary of facts about your product, service, or new business activity. (2) It uses short sentences. (3) It is double spaced, and designed to be easily read. (4) It avoids "selling" words, such as best, leader, top in its class, and top seller. (5) It is dated. (6) It gives a person's name as a contact.

Whether your news release gets printed by the newspaper or magazine or read by the radio station or television station depends on how important the powers that be feel your news release will be for their public. There is an examination period when they determine what effect the news story will have. Make sure that your news item is important! The news release has a better chance for success when it looks professional, has no misspellings, is grammatically correct, and is filled with facts. Save your sales pitch for your mail promotions; include only quality information in your news release.

You will know when the news release is accepted when it is printed or aired. Do not call an editor to see if your news release ran in the last issue of the newspaper. Editors are too busy to report to people on how their news releases fare, but they will remember your name, and when you send another news release, be inclined to throw it in the wastebasket. Many news releases are put there anyway, because thousands of news releases are sent out daily, and only a small percentage will get accepted. However, this is still an excellent way of getting your newsletter known, and the cost of writing and printing up the release, and posting it, is minimal.

Send the news release to many media outlets. Send 100 to 300 news releases to introduce your new publication to magazines, newspapers, and newsletters that are in some way related to the title of your newsletter. For example, if your *Money Management* newsletter targets working men and women, you could send your news release to magazines and newspapers that address this target group. Send the release to radio and television shows that target the same group. You can get a list of the magazines in the *Standard Rate and Data Book* and a list of the newsletters in the *Directory of Newsletters,* both available at your library. When you mail out your release to the newspapers, try to mail it to a particular editor. For example, if your newsletter is on religion, send it to the editor in charge of the religion section of the paper. The *Gale Directory of Publications* gives you the names and addresses of magazines and a listing of each feature editor, complete with phone number. A news release sent to a specific person will be received better than one sent to the name and address of the magazine or newspaper.

The news release will help get you free publicity, and can also get you subscriptions as well. Many people—your inquiries—will write and call you once they hear about you and your newsletter. This is where your publicity and direct mail promotions work together. You send the sales letter, brochure, and order card directly to these people. The news release also serves to take your marketing and public relations to people who would not be in your normal target market.

## Television and radio

Many newsletter owners feel that the only way to get publicity is in magazines and newspapers, that all other media are too difficult to even attempt. This is not true.

Good publicity is timely. The economy is in a recession, a large number of people are unemployed, and many people in their twenties are living at home. Do you have any special knowledge about any of these subjects? Perhaps you can get on a radio or television show by convincing them they would benefit by your appearance. There is always a need for an expert to talk about a timely topic, on very short notice. Be willing to act promptly to get good publicity.

Television can be an important medium for you. Start at the bottom rather than trying to get on a prime time network show. Your local cable station is always looking for guests for talk shows, and many stations are looking for people who have the energy and ideas to start their own shows. Tape your appearances, so that you can send the tapes to cable shows in other areas to add to your audience. Take advantage of the cable shows in your area. Write to the host of a show; tell the host you would like to appear on the show. Include a news release telling about your new publication. Follow up the letter of interest and your news release with a telephone call. Again stress the reasons why the television viewers of the show, and the public in general, will benefit from the information you can offer. Stress the benefits, not to you but to the television viewers. Ask the host of the show, or the programming manager of the show, to set up a booking date. Choose a time convenient to you. Avoid making the television booking close to the time you leave work. You cannot be late for a television show.

Prepare yourself for the show by going over questions the host might ask you. Try to relax in front of the camera; the more relaxed you become, the better your response from the audience. When you answer questions, make certain that the answers focus on the benefits to the viewers. At the end of the program, thank the host for having you on the show. Send a thank-you card the next day to the host or programming manager for having you on the show.

When you do a good job on the show, the producer or programming manager will call you to reappear. All television shows enjoy good guests. When you receive telephone or mail responses from your television program, answer them quickly, thank the callers and writers for their interest, and send them your direct mailings. Start with a cable show, and then approach larger audience shows, until you reach the network show or a show in a large city. Good television publicity works.

Purchasing radio commercials is expensive, and they may miss the mark unless they are aired on exactly the right radio program. The very best radio publicity is to appear as a guest focusing on a subject that relates to your newsletter. For example, an attorney, appearing as a specialist on estate planning, cannot add value to a newsletter on Japanese manufacturing techniques. Appear on the show as a specialist in the same area as your newsletter topic, and ask the host to mention your newsletter by name and to give the audience your address and telephone number. Many guests find that once the interview is over, too little information is given to the audience about the newsletter or how to get more information. Give the audience a way to contact you once the show is over.

Send a sample newsletter, along with your brochure, to the radio stations in your area, specifically directed to the show that can best accommodate your newsletter topic. If your topic is on small business, send it to the talk show that invites guests to discuss small businesses. Dial in to these stations regularly, so that you can avoid sending them information that they recently covered. Radio shows do not want to duplicate a topic no matter how competent the guest might be. Radio shows are rated weekly or monthly, and their survival depends on their ability to stay ahead of their competition. (The radio station can charge more for commercials when their ratings are high.)

Send your publicity material to the producer of the show. Your local library can give you the name of the producer and the name, address, and telephone number of the radio station. If you haven't heard from the producer after a week, call directly. Once the producer is on the phone, sell yourself and your subject idea; give the topic of your newsletter, and the benefits of your ideas for the listeners of the show. *Ask for a booking.* I repeat—*Ask for a booking.* Make it a specific time; make certain you have no conflicts for this time period. Book it on your calendar, and send the producer a thank-you note the next day. A day or two before the appearance date, call the producer or a member of the staff to confirm the date and time. You just earned very valuable publicity, which can add subscriptions and exposure for your newsletter.

Many newsletter owners promote their newsletter by talking with thousands, even hundreds of thousands of people on the radio without even leaving home. How do they do it? They send program producers a news release, a copy of their sales letter, a sample copy of their newsletter, and a cover letter explaining why they would be good talk show guests. Many radio talk programs will accept phone interviews, which means you can talk to an audience of 100,000 people in the comfort of your home. Use this phone interview technique to reach talk programs from Maine to California, from Texas to Minnesota.

*Give something away free.* When you get a chance to appear on a radio program with a large audience, get the names of the listeners to build your list of potential customers. For example, I appeared on a radio talk show that was broadcast to more than thirty states, from

Maine to Illinois, and even to Florida. After about an hour, the host asked me to stay on the show for yet another hour. It was around 1 A.M., and I could visualize listeners all across these states turning off their radios so as to go to sleep. I knew I needed an idea to keep those listeners tuned in. I asked the host, "Can I offer the listeners of the program a free gift?" The host replied on air, "Sure, Bill, what do you have to offer my listeners?" I told the listeners that I would send them a free report on home-based business opportunities if they would send me a large self-addressed stamped envelope. I gave my address over the airways. The response was tremendous. I received more than 180 letters from people in many states. My mailbox was filled for three straight days. The letters thanked me for appearing on the show. When I sent the report to the listeners, I enclosed my sales letter and information on my newsletter as well. The radio program was a huge success. It gave me experience talking to a radio audience, and it helped build my prospect and house lists because I was willing to give something away free. People love free gifts. Remember that in all your newsletter offers, and in all your promotions.

Some guests on radio and television shows talk about their newsletter or book or product, but never connect the potential listener to the newsletter. To be successful, you must describe how people can benefit with the right knowledge at the right time, and persuade your audience that the publication can impact on their lives. One way to do this is to express genuine interest in every question the host asks you, to listen carefully to each call you receive on the phone lines, and to refer to your newsletter often. Callers really care about your subject, or they would not call. Make each caller feel special. People like to be treated this way. So do you. My style emphasizes caring about others, helping them to reach their goals, and being positive about their ability to succeed. I have developed this style over the years, and I feel comfortable using it. You will develop a style that will work for you. Avoid trying to copy another's style; it may not work for you. When your style is successful, your callers will remember you and your newsletter and will feel positively about both.

Show enthusiasm for your subject, and your newsletter, and become your number 1 supporter. For example, there is an author who writes books on free government publications, and how to use the numerous free services paid for by the taxpayers in America. This author is so enthusiastic that he almost falls out of his chair in his efforts to communicate his enthusiasm to others. He raises his voice and gets all excited about his subject. He gets people to pay attention to him because of this extreme enthusiasm. He is a star guest. Many radio and television shows will call on him to fill in when another guest fails to appear. He is asked over and over again to appear on show after show. This author takes great pains to show how the information in his publication benefits others, and how much money, time, and effort they can save by reading his books. Try to use some of these techniques when publicizing your newsletter.

## Magazine articles and newsletter reviews

Many newsletters can be sold by getting exposure from a magazine article or a review of your newsletter by a writer in your field. You can expose your newsletter to reviewers by sending a news release and sample copy to magazines or specialized newspapers in the field. Request a review of your own newsletter, or suggest that an article be written reviewing several newsletters in the field.

People need information, and to get this valuable information they rely on magazines and newsletters. For example, a recent article in a Wisconsin magazine discusses new opportunities for starting a business in today's competitive atmosphere. The article gives a list of newsletters and books on the subject.

You might want to write an article yourself if you have the time, information, and interest. You can write or call your local newspaper or magazine and sell your article idea to them. When they decide to do your article, your newsletter will be mentioned in the byline— more free publicity! A copy of the article can be included in your direct mail package.

## Speaking engagements

Many groups, such as Kiwanis, Rotary, Exchange, and Women's Business Clubs, use speakers to inform and entertain their members. Many of these groups are located in your home town, or in the town or city in which you work. This is a pleasant way to get exposure for yourself and your newsletter, and each talk you make leads to other speaking engagements. I just finished speaking to my local Kiwanis club, and the president of the Rotary in a local town outside of Boston, who was present, asked me to address his group. A talk lasts only about 15–20 minutes, and you can choose any topic that will interest the audience. When you finish the talk, you can ask for questions. Before you sit down, thank the members for the opportunity to appear before their group, and state that you look forward to returning. Now tell them that you have copies of your newsletter with you, and that anyone interested in getting more information and a free newsletter can come to the front of the room at the end of the program. Take their names, so that you can mail your newsletter samples, sales letters, and reply cards to the members of the group. Hand out business cards. As part of the compensation for your speech, many clubs give you a complimentary lunch and a small token gift, such as a coffee cup or nail cutter with the logo of the club or organization. Call or write your local club, and express your interest in speaking to their group. This is an excellent way of gaining exposure.

## Run your own seminars

After you have spoken at a number of clubs and organizations your confidence level will be high. You will be ready to set up your own seminar on a topic that in some fashion relates to your newsletter subject. You can hold your seminar in a local business school, community college, college, or university. Choose a subject that will attract an audience. Will your seminar help the students make more money? Will your seminar teach them new ways to look at themselves and their lives? Will your seminar take a basic subject, and look at it in a different, relevant, worthwhile manner? When you feel a seminar idea will benefit you and increase your newsletter exposure, it is time to hold one.

Call your local community college, ask for the division of continuing education department, and ask to set up an interview to discuss your seminar idea. Do an outline showing the various subjects you will discuss in your seminar. For example, a seminar on money management might include the following topics:

Financial planning
Compound interest
Common stock
Preferred stock
Mutual funds
Money market funds
Bonds

Corporate bonds

Retirement planning

College funding

Limited partnership

Your personal financial plan

Tell the representative of the college why you want to do the seminar, how it will benefit the students, how the material is relevant, and why you should be the person to direct the seminar. Give all the reasons why your education and background fully prepare you to teach. Make certain that you mention the fact that you publish a monthly newsletter, and leave a copy of the newsletter with the representative together with your outline for the seminar. Call the representative in about a week if you fail to get an answer. Once selected, work hard to get a good evaluation from your students. This is valuable exposure and excellent publicity, and you get paid for it as well. I started to do seminars about 15 years ago. I also founded and directed many seminars in schools and colleges. Once you get a good subject, students will flock to your seminars. To keep them coming will require hard work and intense preparation. You must always look for new ways to communicate your material.

## Let others sell your newsletter

You can only sell so many newsletters yourself. Why not permit others to help sell your publication? For example, a small publishing company selling business books might want to add your newsletter to its catalog, and any subscriptions received will be given to you less 50 percent commission. For example, let's say your newsletter sells for $59 per year, and when the small publisher sells one subscription, he will send you a check for $29. You benefit in two ways: You get free access to people who might never have heard of or seen your newsletter, and you get new paid subscriptions, without paying advertising costs. Write to any small publishers, business associates, or mail-order owners who put out a brochure or catalog with products and services that complement your newsletter.

## Write a letter to the editor

Using the letter to the editor section of your newspaper to help you learn to write is important. But this is also a powerful way to communicate your expertise and understanding of a particular subject. Research your subject well, and write about it in a convincing manner. When your letter is published, make certain that you cut it out and that you note the publication's name and the date of publication on it. You might reproduce it and use it in your publicity program. Some newsletter owners who write many letters to the editor collect them in a scrapbook, which they present at seminars and at special events, trade shows, and speaking events.

Letters to the editor can attract subscribers. For example, one newsletter owner received a telephone call in response to a letter to the editor. The caller said, "You should write a newsletter on selling to the Middle East countries." The newsletter owner replied, "I am the founder of a newsletter on that very subject. Would you like me to send you a sample copy of my newsletter?" This is an excellent example of public relations at work. Use any opportunity to communicate your knowledge and interest in your topic.

## Print up business cards

A business card can be a public relations star for you. Some newsletter owners use the masthead of their newsletter on their business cards, and give the owner's name, full address, and telephone number. You can print up to 500 business cards for about $25. Enclose your business card in your direct mail package. Send your business card to radio and television producers and to newspaper and magazine editors. Have some business cards on hand at all times.

## Put your name in directories

Many newsletter owners believe that they must pay for a directory listing or purchase an advertisement in the directories in order to get a listing. This is not correct. Many directories give listings for free. The directories are sold to people interested in the names and addresses in them, and the publishers of the directories earn money from these sales. Some potential subscribers will read directories to get ideas about newsletters and their contents. Some examples of directories are *Oxbridge Directory of Newsletters* (Oxbridge Comm.), *Newsletters in Print* (Gale Research), and *Encyclopedia of Associations* (Gale Research).

## Ask for article ideas

Some newsletter owners ask writers to send articles and article ideas to them to review, with the possibility that they might use them in their publication. Some of these newsletters are listed in writers' magazines, and the listing is free of charge. You will get writers asking for sample copies, and others requesting information on subscription rates and newsletter contents. Answer all inquiries and enclose your sales letter and order card. The key to successful publicity is to get the word out about your newsletter and how easily it can be ordered.

## Donate your newsletter

Send your newsletter to nursing homes, hospitals, colleges, universities, or local and regional libraries to expose it to people who would not otherwise know about it. One newsletter owner in Maine sent a newsletter subscription to the educational television station in Boston, Massachusetts, to be auctioned off during a fund-raising program. This gave worthwhile publicity to the newsletter; thousands, perhaps hundreds of thousands of viewers, learned about the newsletter. Some viewers might call the show to get the newsletter's full name and address. These people can be included in your prospect list for future mailings should they decide not to subscribe right away. Keep asking subscribers how they heard about your publication.

## Put on a product and service fair

Design a fair to attract the people who would order your newsletter. A newsletter owner on the subject of franchising, hired a hall, called the fair "Franchising Showcase," and sold space to businesses offering franchises, and those selling to franchises. It also included lawyers, accountants, builders, and contractors interested in new franchises. Sample newsletters and information on the newsletter were handed out. The fair was a success. The newsletter owner sold many subscriptions, and made others aware that a publication on franchising was available. Remember to be fair; be careful not to give special attention in your newsletter to people purchasing space in your fair.

## Approach those in the news

Cut out interesting articles that give you valuable leads about people, new businesses, and events that would benefit from your newsletter.

Who is being promoted at work? Who started a business related to your newsletter? Who was recently elected to the presidency of your local service organization? Who recently graduated from school, college, or a special seminar? For example, I was recently featured in my local paper, and a few days after the article appeared, I received telephone calls, letters, and comments from people on the street. Anyone who is featured or even mentioned in some small way will expect to hear about the article from others and, at the same time, will be receptive to new offers for products and services. When you read newspapers and magazines, keep a scissors close by to cut out leads. Put them in a "leads" folder, and mail the leads information, followed by a call. Once your newsletter grows, you can hire a clipping service to do this for you.

## Public relations is a year-long process

Good public relations is much like exercising in that, you have to keep on doing it in order for it to be effective. Good public relations starts on January 1 and goes right through to December 31. People look forward to mail offers in January, February, and March, but will read them all year long. You can speak to business and service groups all year long. You can hand out business cards all year long. Like the electricity in your home or apartment, your public relations program should keep running all year long.

Some customers will be reached by the small-space advertisement in the business journal; others will be reached by a well-timed news release in the local or technical newspaper or magazine. Often business people don't realize that public relations is only part of your marketing plan. This is a well-kept secret. Most business people use either advertisements or news releases, but only a few, aware business owners know the value of working both the marketing and the public relations together, getting the best from both, and working each plan, all year long, from the cold days in January, to the windy days of April, to the humid days of July, to the frost in October, to the soft flakes of snow in December.

## Test your public relations ideas

Successful newsletters know how to get good, free, workable public relations, month after month, year after year. When you get a publicity idea that works, never—I repeat, never—stop using it until it stops working. No matter what comments you hear from others, continue to write letters to the editor, to give seminars, even free seminars as long as they are getting you newsletter subscriptions. Keep testing, and when you find the technique that works for you, simply do it over and over.

## Summary

Public relations are free. Public relations opportunities are everywhere, from guest appearances on television shows to invitations to address a meeting of the local service club. Design a public relations program to reach your market. A news release opens up the doors and sells subscriptions. Appear on a cable television show or radio program to reach your market. Persist in making contacts and handing out your material. Get your newsletter reviewed. Conduct a seminar at a college or high school. Ask others to sell your newsletter in their catalog or mailings. Write letters to your local newspaper editor. Buy and hand out business cards. Get your newsletter listed in directories. Donate your publication to worthy people and businesses. Put on a product and service fair. Follow up on valuable leads to sell your newsletter. Keep testing your newsletter public relations ideas.

Now let's look at some ways to manage your business for success.

# 13

# Managing your newsletter business

Successful newsletters are made and not born. Success is the result not only of planning the right topic, developing a content, doing a mission statement, completing a golden contract with your subscribers, producing a quality publication, marketing and publicizing your newsletter, but of managing your newsletter to make all the hard work and planning pay off for you.

Managing is keeping your customers satisfied, so that they not only keep buying your newsletter, but also tell their friends, who buy and then tell others. Management is keeping the important parts of your business under control, so that your best efforts can shine through to your customer.

Generally, your newsletter management activities will be in three basic areas: newsletter quality control, customer service, and record keeping and analysis to keep your newsletter profitable and ahead of the competition. Good management, like good marketing, is a continuous process, and goes beyond the weekly or monthly meeting with your staff. Good management is taking your stethoscope and checking the heart rate of your business. Is the business healthy and strong? Is the heart beat regular, and strong enough to accept strain in the future? Good management is taking readings on the important parts of the business so that you can keep your business vital and emerging. This chapter will explore management techniques in the newsletter business.

## Be customer-oriented

Your customer is the most important person in your business. The customer is the reason for your newsletter. The customer is doing you a favor by subscribing to your newsletter. When your customer signed up for your newsletter, it was a temporary situation, there was no long-term contract to continue to subscribe. Most customers will sign up for only one year.

You must earn the customer's trust, not only by producing the quality newsletter, but by giving superb customer service. Good management is making certain that minimum errors occur with each subscriber, so that when the decision is made for possible renewals, it will be in your favor.

Good customer service is making each customer feel like the most important person in the world. Forget about techniques to service 80 percent of your customers; give the service that will make 100 percent of your customers happy. A good example of customer service committal is L. L. Bean, the successful mail-order business from Maine, which treats everyone—the caller on the phone, the person writing a letter, and the visitor to the store—with dignity and gives the impression that every person is a special customer for L. L. Bean. This customer-service philosophy is backed up by a 100 percent satisfaction guarantee. A special telephone number for customer service operates 24 hours, 7 days a week. The foundation of L. L. Bean's customer service is their 100 percent guarantee. The customer must be satisfied in every way or the merchandise is replaced or the purchase price is refunded. Good customer relations offers the customers the best possible product or service possible.

Good customer relations is solving a customer's problems before the problem grows into resentment and misunderstanding. One newsletter owner uses a technique of taking a complaint, and dealing with it right away to solve it promptly. For example, a subscriber from

South Dakota wrote to her about not receiving the previous two issues of the newsletter, threatening to terminate the subscription. The newsletter owner immediately telephoned the subscriber to apologize for the inconvenience and to assure the subscriber that copies of the missing newsletters had been sent by first-class mail that day. The subscriber was pleased with the immediate response, and the owner saved a subscriber to her newsletter.

Customer relations in the twenty-first century do not take the customer for granted. In your business, continue to take a reading of your customer. What does the subscriber expect from your publication? Are you delivering this information to your customer? Since your customer is changing continuously, you must implement the changes to meet your customers' new needs. Never expect your customer's needs to change to meet your publication's specifications. You risk your customer walking right out the door to a competitor. Remember that your customer has the power to do whatever he or she decides to do.

Customer relations means keeping an open communication network with your customer so that customer can tell you how your publication can improve. For example, a newsletter owner from North Carolina doing a newsletter on careers was asked by a subscriber to do something on bringing employers together with job seekers. This idea was developed, and an issue was devoted to listing jobs in the area. It was a major success.

Customer relations means knowing the value of the customer's perception of you and your business. When a customer feels that you are delivering a publication that is the best in the field, or a publication that is getting better and better, or that is making an effort to get better, you may get a renewal and recommendations to potential customers.

Customer relations means keeping an open mind and an open eye on what the competition is doing for their customers. Publication A is giving rebates and doing extensive surveys on subscriber needs and evaluations. What do you plan to do to compete? For example, one large, well-known newsletter is offering free gifts with each paid subscription. To motivate the customer to continue to pay for a subscription, this newsletter is offering free reports with timely information in each report. How can you compete with a competitor who has been in the business for a long time, and is using different methods to hold the business? Good management means evaluating each situation, and making a decision that will work for you. It does not mean that you must copy the techniques used by others. A technique that will succeed for one publication might fall flat for another.

Customer relations of the twenty-first century take into account that everything in life—the economy, stocks, housing, construction, arts, even consumer moods—has a cycle. Cycles have a life—a beginning, growth stage, leveling off, and then decline. Your customer also has a life cycle; many studies show that the average subscriber has a five-year life. This means that the subscriber is likely to keep buying for only five years. One newsletter owner reviews his customers regularly, to determine how many near-to-end customers are on the customer list, and what steps are necessary to keep them on the customer list. Some newsletter owners try to add one new subscriber to every five or six on their subscriber list.

Good customer relations start before the sale is made, and never end. Customer satisfaction can make or break your business and the success of your publication. Make every effort to treat your customers with respect and fairness.

## Know your publication

You cannot manage any business unless you know the business you are in. In the newsletter business you are not simply selling words on white paper; you are selling important information to help your subscribers compete in an ever-changing world. You are selling success. You are selling ideas to help your readers beat their competition. You are selling hope for the future. View your publication in the broadest sense, so that you can position the publication in a special way and can examine all possible benefits together.

Your publication must fulfill your image in order to receive the acceptance of today's difficult-to-please consumer. It must not only fulfill your initial goals, mission statement, and golden contract, but it must also perform to the highest degree. As a manager you cannot measure everything, but the most important thing you must measure is the product itself, and the performance of the publication. One side of the performance of your newsletter is the product itself. A format for a performance evaluation of your newsletter is shown at the top of the following pages.

| | Excellent | Good | Fair | Poor |
|---|---|---|---|---|
| How is the appearance? | | | | |
| How is it written? | | | | |
| Does it communicate effectively? | | | | |
| Does the reader get value for money? | | | | |
| Is the material new and exciting? | | | | |
| Would you subscribe to this newsletter? | | | | |

Your publication evaluation is important and should be done on a regular basis to make any changes necessary to maintain a high standard. This is your opportunity to measure the quality of your publication, and become your own quality control expert, or quality checker.

The other side of measuring your newsletter's performance is the real world, the only place that counts—the total amount of sales generated by your newsletter. Your total sales is the total amount of subscribers you sold during the last year. You cannot count the newsletters you donate or those you give away to your friends, associates, or businesses. Sales are essential to stay in your business. Set a goal for total sales in your business for the first year. For example, if your newsletter sells for $36 per year, and you want 1000 customers the first year, the total sales will be $36,000. This is an excellent example of the concept that newsletters are made not born. You will have to go out and sell the newsletter to make it into the success you know it can become. Every three months you should go over your total sales, and determine whether or not you are on target to meet your sales goal for the year. If your performance is not strong enough, you must set up a strategy to get more sales. Perhaps your marketing and public relations programs are not working hard enough to increase your sales. Perhaps you need to send more sales letters out to your prospect list. You might need to spend time telephoning people who ex-

pressed an interest in subscribing but failed to do so. When you find
the sales beginning to taper off, it's time for some action. The sale of
your newsletter is the engine of your business, and the fuel to run the
engine is the quality product and the marketing and public relations
programs.

An Ohio owner started a newsletter on the crafts business, and
the quality of the newsletter was fine. It was one of the best newsletters in the field, and the sales looked promising at first. Then sales
dropped, because many subscribers who had signed up for the two-
month trial subscription did not send in their payments for the full
subscription. They simply lost interest in the publication. The newsletter owner decided to add an incentive to the subscribers to get
them to pay for a full subscription. The incentive was a free booklet
on the 10 most profitable craft ideas of the twenty-first century. The
response was excellent, and now sales are back on track. Good management is knowing your publication and business so well that you
can take problem situations and turn them into opportunities for success.

A newsletter owner from Chicago found that her problem was
turning subscribers into renewals. She had healthy new sales, but the
renewal rate was not strong enough. When she reviewed her renewal
process, she found that it didn't start early enough before the subscription terminated. By starting a full two weeks earlier, the renewals
increased, and improved the overall sales for the year. Good management is reviewing the newsletter regularly and making the changes
necessary to improve your performance.

## Keep good records

Good managers know their publication and business because they
keep records that show them how the newsletter is performing and
what changes are happening within the business. One of the most important records you keep will be the detailed information profiles of
your subscribers. This information will tell you about how all the
other parts of your business are working. A customer profile card can
be used to track each customer. This card can tell you whether the
subscriber responded to an advertisement from the energy magazine,
or to the sales letter to the mailing list of energy-device buyers. Did
you use any special sales promotion to obtain the subscription? Is the
subscriber part of the market you targeted in the beginning days of
your newsletter? What date will you start your renewal process with

this customer? The customer profile will be able to give you valuable information about how your sales are being generated, and what public relations techniques are working for you. Once you determine a method that works, continue to use it until it loses its appeal. Some newsletter owners keep these customer profiles on computer files, while others keep them on cards in a fireproof file cabinet. Make certain that these records are kept up to date and that renewal packages are sent out on a monthly basis to customers whose subscriptions are running out. Use the format shown below to create a customer profile.

```
Name_____     Address_____

City_____     State_____ ZIP_____

Tel. #_____

                                              Direct     Other
Date                                          Mail       Pub.
Order                             Mailing     Pack       Rel.
Rec'd.   Magazine  Advertisement  List
____     _____  _____   ____        ____       ____

Date entered on mailing list_____

Date for renewal and renewal package_____

Will follow up again_____

Date paid_____  Check #_____

Remarks_____
```

## Buy quality services and supplies

The newsletter business may require you to purchase services, such as writing, editing, and proofreading, and supplies, such as paper, computer software, and office items. Buy locally from people who can give you good service and can back up their products. For example, one newsletter owner bought an important part for his word processor from a mail-order computer supplier, and when he had a problem with the part, had difficulty getting it repaired correctly and on time. The newsletter owner missed a deadline because of his problems with the supplier. By dealing with quality local suppliers, your turnaround time will be shorter. In the newsletter business, time is money. Take the time to evaluate your purchases. Do you get good value for the money spent? Do you get service when there is a problem? Your suppliers should earn your business. Keep those suppliers that are working for you, and terminate those that are not doing the job.

## The profit and loss statement

Your success will come from the bottom line, and the bottom line in the newsletter business, as in any other business, is the difference between sales and expenses. At the end of the year, you will total up your sales for the year. During the first year, your sales will be primarily subscriptions. Let's say that sales totaled $36,000, the result of 1000 subscriptions, and that total expenses were $26,000. Your profit is the difference between the sales of $36,000 and the $26,000 in expenses. Your profit is $10,000. Your tax return must pay taxes on the $10,000 and not the $36,000. An income statement is shown below.

**Income Statement:**
**The Newsletter on Crafts**
**December 31, 2000**

| | | |
|---|---|---|
| Sales from subscriptions | | $36,000 |
| Expenses | | |
| Printing | $6,000 | |
| Mailing postage | 4,000 | |
| Office supplies | 2,000 | |
| Marketing costs | 5,000 | |
| Advertising | 6,000 | |
| Legal and accounting | 3,000 | |
| Total expenses | | $26,000 |
| Net income | | $10,000 |

There are two basic ways to increase your profits: One is to increase revenue by selling more subscriptions, the other is to decrease expenses. Good management reviews the revenue and expenses monthly to make certain that they are in line with your expectations and goals. You need revenue to keep the money coming into the business, to pay your obligations, and to continue to print the newsletter.

## Cash flow

Cash flow is essential to keep your business open and growing. You might be making a profit on paper, but unless the money keeps coming into your business from subscriptions sold, you will be forced to borrow money to run the business. Your break-even point is $26,000; you need $2,167 a month to run the business. Try to run the business on its own by selling subscriptions, renewals, and multi-year subscriptions. One newsletter owner was on the point of going to the bank for a second loan during the first year of his business, when he decided to get on the phone to collect overdue subscriptions, work harder on renewals, and stress multi-year subscriptions to his customers. Put the price of the multi-year subscriptions right on the newsletter. Multi-year subscriptions are for two or more years. For example, instead of collecting for a one-year subscription of $39, sell a three-year subscription for $95, and win a long-time subscriber. This is a double win because you get $95 up front and the customer saves $22. There will be no need to send a renewal to this customer for almost three years, which saves money for you.

When you offer the "bill me" terms to customers, some will be slow in paying. After sending out your first invoice for a yearly subscription, wait for two weeks. If the money has not been received, send another invoice, and clearly tell the subscriber that if payment is not received promptly, service will be terminated. State this clearly, but diplomatically. See the example below.


Dear Subscriber:

Your payment has not been received for your *The Real Estate Newsletter* subscription.

Perhaps you mislaid the invoice, or simply forgot it during your busy life style.

Please take a few seconds to pay the enclosed invoice, so that I can send you our next fact-filled *Real Estate Newsletter.*

Sincerely,


Betty Smith, Publisher/Owner


P.S.: A *free gift,* a new report on *New England Real Estate in 2001* will be sent once your check is received.

Once you sent out the overdue letter, wait a week to ten days for a response. If you fail to get the payment, make one more attempt and then stop sending your newsletter to this nonsubscriber. You might want to follow up with a direct mail package in the future. Many news-letters and magazines rent their list of expires and nonsubscribers, people who decided not to continue for some reason. Don't make the mistake of assuming that people who became nonsubscribers are too difficult to satisfy, and that your publication or service is not at fault. Something motivated them to act in this manner. As the manager and owner, you must do some research when you have too many nonsubscribers or expires. What motivated them to leave your publi-cation? Is the quality of the publication at fault? Is it priced too high? Is a certain group of people, such as doctors, accountants, sales peo-ple, or engineers becoming expires or nonsubscribers? Analyze the reasons why and take action to reverse the trend. Good management spots trends and acts on them.

Don't make the mistake of giving your product away for free. When Sandy Jones decides to terminate her trial subscription to your newsletter, don't take it personally. Don't write to her and ask that she accept the newsletter free of charge. You have to work hard to pro-duce a quality newsletter, and you deserve the profit and the recog-nition from running your business. People will pay for a quality prod-uct. Expect some resistance, but with good service and a regularly issued quality newsletter you will succeed.

## Develop a good public image

The image you develop is based on a number of important factors. One factor is the customer relations program discussed earlier in this chapter; another is the quality of your publication, and how you com-pete in your field. Your advertising program must be rolled out along with your public relations program, and you must fulfill all the things you say you will do. For example, if you say you will send out a monthly newsletter on the first day of each month, make certain you do so. If you say you will give a special gift on payment of the sub-scription, send it out promptly. People judge you on your actions. Your image will be developed in the first 18–24 months of your busi-ness. Your positive actions can establish a favorable image to build on in the months and years ahead.

## Go the extra mile

Your newsletter's success is going to be determined by how much you are willing to do for your subscribers. Will you do extra research in a particular area to help them? For example, one newsletter in Washington, D.C. invites subscribers to write with questions on bills in the legislature; they check on the status of the bill for the subscriber. Other newsletters offer advice on specific areas free of charge for subscribers. Review your newsletter field and the needs of your subscribers to offer the most relevant and worthwhile services possible.

## Review your marketing program regularly

A newsletter owner in Minnesota calls his editor and assistant together every three months to review the effectiveness of advertisements. How many dollars in sales does each advertisement receive? What magazines are working for the newsletter? In the same meeting, the direct mail package is examined fully. The sales letter is read out loud, with the AIDA process in mind, to see if it is communicating to the reader correctly. Nothing happens until a sale is made. If your direct mail package is not getting the sales for you, revise it. Or make a new one, with a new theme. Use stronger emotional motives, such as how to earn more money, get promoted, and beat the competition to increase the sales. You must work on your marketing program all year round.

## Beware of free loaders

Some people will write to claim that they sent you a check a number of weeks before, yet never received their newsletter. This is the oldest trick in the book, and it works because some people never check their records, and just send the publication to the nonpayer free of charge. Go back to your cash deposits, which should list the names of the people who subscribed in that time period, and also check your customer profile cards discussed earlier in this chapter to see whether a subscription was paid for, and what check number was used. If you cannot find a customer profile for this customer, there is a strong possibility that this individual did not pay for the newsletter. Send a letter such as the following.

Dear Sir:

Thank you for your letter of April 13th, and your request for our news-letter *The Newsletter on Theater Arts*.

Please send me a copy of both sides of your cancelled check. Once I receive it, I can send out your newsletter right away.

Thank you for your interest in our publication.

Sincerely,


Holly Burnside
Publisher/Owner


Another group of people who might try to get the newsletter for free is the group of people who want the newsletter sent to them on a complimentary basis. These people will tell you they run a not-for-profit group and would benefit by your newsletter, and might even give you some publicity free for sending a complimentary copy to them. Be careful. Many complimentary copies never, never turn into subscriptions. Unless you screen the complimentary copies carefully, your public relations effect will be minimal. Consider giving them a one- or two-issue trial subscription, and then ask for the full subscription order. Many new owners are lenient with complimentary copies, but once they find out the cost of printing, mailing, addressing, and keeping records current, they are not as eager to hand out complimentary copies.

## Keep an eye on your image

You manage your image, not your printer, your artist, or your employees. Your subscribers will judge you by how professional your newsletter looks compared to others in the field. Never run down the competition. Just do your job better than the others, and keep doing this over and over.

## Train someone to fill in for you

Too often the newsletter owner feels indispensable, that no one can do the job as well as the one-person owner. The owner works hard to get the newsletter out on time and builds the business over time.

What happens if the newsletter owner gets sick with the flu? Or goes into the hospital for surgery? What happens if an emergency takes the owner out of state? You may need someone to take over the reins of your business, and if you fail to train someone, you will be out of luck, and your subscribers will lose in the end. One newsletter owner from New York, with many years of experience running and owning newsletters, recommends training a free-lance writer to prepare a newsletter issue, taking the free-lancer through the editing, proofreading, preparation for printing, printing, and mailing processes. When you are going to be away for a few issues, make sure that the free-lancer understands your expectations. Evaluate the free-lancer, so that necessary changes can be made, and then your results will be better.

## Be consistent

Your customers judge you on your ability to keep your publication and your services consistent from one day to the next, one month to the next. A customer confident in your ability to maintain standards will also feel confident about doing business with you.

The best way to monitor consistency is to look at your business from a customer's point of view. Would you as a customer buy from a company that offers your services and publications? Why or why not? Asking this important question permits you to look at business from the other side of the desk. It will help you to examine some areas of your business that need work to keep your newsletter up to the expectations of the customers and up with the competition. Keep asking yourself why your customers should buy from you.

## Concentrate on essential elements

A newsletter owner in the personal computer field claims his success is the result of concentrating all his efforts on putting out the best newsletter in his field. Most of his energy is spent researching the latest development and reporting it to his subscribers. By concentrating on improving his newsletter, few competitors are tempted to break into the field, and any new competitors find it very difficult to get a foot in the door. His is a quality newsletter, with a strong following.

Marketing and public relations is important, but it is difficult to sell an average or below-average product. A quality product will sell over and over again, so put your time and energy where it belongs, right into the newsletter itself. Make your newsletter the best in its field, and you will reap the harvest.

Continue to concentrate on the reasons why you started the newsletter in the first place. A New England owner of a newsletter on mutual funds felt that she could make better use of charts and graphs than other newsletters in the field. She felt that the creative use of charts and graphs coupled with excellent reporting on trends in various industries could establish her niche in the field. At last count, her subscription list is at 575 and climbing.

*Strive for credibility.* Do what you say you are going to do is the basis of credibility. One newsletter owner from Florida sent out a sales letter claiming that he was going to publish a newsletter on the fastest-growing industries, combined with the best careers of the future. Many subscribers wanted and needed this information.

After three or four issues, the owner did not fulfill his responsibilities, and many subscribers either cancelled or wrote to the owner about the delay in delivering on his promise. The owner took some action to get the newsletter back on track, but much credibility was lost. Do everything possible to fulfill your promises; once you lose your credibility, it will be difficult to regain it.

## Summary

Customer-oriented business succeeds. Customer relations means understanding the complete process of purchasing a newsletter. Get to know your publication fully. Sales are essential to success. Know your break-even point. Turn subscribers into renewals. Keep records on your customers' profiles. Buy quality services and supplies. Remember that the profit and loss statement is your key scorecard. Bill your customers on time, and be aggressive, but gentle, with slow payers. Work hard on your public image. Go the extra mile. Review your marketing program regularly. Beware of people who want free subscriptions. Train someone to fill in for you in an emergency. Concentrate on essential elements. Be consistent so that people can feel comfortable.

Now let's sum up.

# 14
# Summing up

Congratulations for reading this book until the end. Now is the time to sum up the essential points so that you can make a fast start in your business. Nothing happens in life until you make it happen. Far too many newsletter owners and potential newsletter owners delayed until someone else started a similar newsletter and beat them to the punch. Strike when the iron is hot. The greatest benefit of producing your own newsletter is seeing your words and ideas in print. Your confidence grows, you get better and better, and you branch out into many other projects.

What are the essential points to get you started in the newsletter business?

## Setting up a home-based operation

1. You only need a typewriter or computer to start.
2. You should choose a quiet area of your house or apartment.
3. Write each day to develop your writing skills.
4. Your writing, and freedom to write, is protected by the U.S. Constitution.
5. Many famous entrepreneurs started at home.

6. Good time management is necessary to get the newsletter written.

7. Check with your lawyer for insurance and legal advice.

8. Check with your town or city clerk's office for any licenses required to start your business.

9. You must pay taxes on any profits you earn in the business.

10. Keep good financial records.

## Choosing a good newsletter subject

11. The best subject for you is your hobby, occupation, or main interest.

12. Match your interests with the needs of a special group.

13. Your subject must be personal to you.

14. Know how a newsletter differs from other publications.

15. Read other newsletters.

16. Know the types of newsletter available to you.

17. Choose a simple newsletter idea in the beginning.

18. Research your competition in your subject area.

19. Look at the market, the people who will buy from you.

20. Put the newsletter and the market together.

21. Target your market.

22. Choose a name for your newsletter.

## Making your newsletter essential reading

23. Develop a sharp focus in your newsletter.

24. A quality newsletter gets subscriptions and renewals.

25. Write a mission statement for your newsletter.

26. The newsletter customer has a bill of rights.

27. The golden contract considers consumers' rights and power.

28. Develop your own strategy.

29. Do your own editorial calendar.

30. Do your own newsletter evaluation.

31. Follow your instincts.
32. You are the editorial and marketing director.
33. Look at the newsletter from the customer's point of view.

## Choosing the content of your newsletter

34. Your content includes subjects, elements, and topics.
35. Become an expert in your newsletter field.
36. Write the newsletter yourself.
37. Choose the content most deserving of your customers.
38. Watch excessive content changes.
39. Choose a theme each issue.

## Writing a winning newsletter

40. Write about a subject you know very well.
41. Keep copy moving along.
42. Accept feedback and criticism.
43. Write every chance you get.
44. Do a complete first draft.
45. Avoid jargon.
46. Underline sparingly.

## Editing and proofreading your newsletter

47. Editing requires knowledge of the subject.
48. Good editing watches copy flow.
49. Good editing has standards.
50. A proofreader looks for spelling errors, missing commas, and wrong names in photographs.
51. A proofreader saves embarrassment.
52. You have responsibility for proofreading accuracy.

## Designing your newsletter

53. The foundation of your newsletter is your format.
54. Choose a format and masthead that best represent your image.

55. Logos are important in your newsletter.

56. The type you use affects your image.

57. Use pull quotes.

58. Strive for consistency.

## Printing and mailing your newsletter

59. Put essential graphic elements together.

60. Hire the best possible printer.

61. Choose the best paper color for your newsletter.

62. Evaluate the printing job before paying for it.

63. Do your own mailing for experience.

64. Newsletters should be sent first-class mail.

65. Charge more for foreign subscriptions.

66. Do a profit and loss analysis for each mailing.

67. Request permission to mail second class.

68. Monitor the weight for all mailings.

## Selling your newsletter

69. Marketing takes insight, energy, and persistence.

70. Nothing happens until a sales letter is made.

71. Make your sales letter work for you.

72. Use the AIDA formula.

73. Use an order card and brochure.

74. Price your newsletter based on your costs.

75. Hit the target directly.

76. Your mailing list is essential.

77. Conduct a test mailing.

78. Use small-space advertisements to build your house list.

79. Advertise in magazines that are aimed at your target market.

80. Make a marketing budget.

81. Get to know your marketing mix.

82. Marketing is everything, and for everyone.

## Using public relations techniques

83. Public relations is a marketing tool.

84. Use the free promotion technique—the news release.

85. Consider television and radio promotion for your newsletter.

86. Get your newsletter reviewed by newspapers and magazines.

87. Speak at Rotary, Kiwanis, service, and professional groups.

88. Run your own seminars.

89. Write a letter to the editor of your newspaper.

90. Print business cards for yourself.

91. Develop your own style.

92. Put your newsletter's name in directories.

93. Donate your newsletter.

94. Put on a product and service fair.

95. Put your newspaper to work to get subscription leads.

96. Include your telephone number on all correspondence.

97. Public relations is a year-round process.

98. Combine public relations with your marketing program.

99. Public relations is free.

## Managing your business

100. Newsletters are made, not born.

101. Become consumer-oriented to succeed.

102. Good customer relations is a 365-day-a-year process.

103. Solve your customers' problems first.

104. Never take your important customer for granted.

105. Your customer's perception of you is everything.

106. Get to know your customer cycle, and keep selling.

107. Know your publication fully.

108. Evaluate the product often.

109. Review your profit and loss statement.

110. Keep records.
111. Know who buys your newsletter subscriptions.
112. Buy quality products and services.
113. Keep your cash flowing.
114. Selling is not enough; collect your money.
115. Maintain a strong public image.
116. Do the extra service to keep your subscribers.
117. Watch out for people who want free newsletters.
118. Good management trains others.
119. Keep a consistent quality newsletter issue after issue.
120. Concentrate on the reasons why you wanted to start the newsletter.
121. Strive and keep your credibility.
122. Give more than the competition.
123. Fulfill all your promises.
124. Good luck and happy newslettering!

# Appendixes

# Appendix A

# The most commonly asked questions

**Q.** How do I pick the best newsletter topic for me?

**A.** Read Chapter 2 again. Choose a subject you know and feel excited about. Choose a subject that has the potential to grow in the 1990s, such as a segment of the service economy, health topics, and modern communications.

**Q.** Do you suggest I just try a subject and see if it will work?

**A.** No, you cannot just try a subject; a subject must be right for you. Starting a newsletter is hard work, and to turn a profit for a quality newsletter that is geared to a specific market will take at least two years.

**Q.** Can I sell other services and products to build my revenue while subscription revenues build over the first two or three years?

**A.** Yes, back issues of your newsletter, seminars, books, and special reports can be sold successfully, but these items cannot replace a quality newsletter, which will become the reason why people buy your other services and publications. Put your full interest, energy, and focus into your newsletter to make it the best in the field. One newsletter owner from Iowa puts out a newsletter on marketing, which is published bi-monthly, sells for $48 per year, and includes information on his products and services. The 30 pages of the newsletter are filled with important information, giving the subscriber his or her money's worth. Don't worry about selling related products until your newsletter becomes a quality publication, and subscriptions are selling strongly. You will succeed when each issue is better than the previous one. People will renew when the product is top quality and meets their needs.

**Q.** I'm not sure about giving the time and effort necessary for a newsletter. Since I am a professional, will a newsletter help my practice? If so, how will it help?

**A.** A doctor in Miami started a newsletter to give his patients current information about his field between their visits. A speech therapist started a newsletter for her patients and associates, and it is growing strongly year after year. An investment adviser in New England started a newsletter to keep his clients updated on investment opportunities and changes in the field. Two consultants from Boston recently started a newsletter for corporations to show how business, parents, and educators can work together to improve education. After a slow start, the newsletter has 10,000 subscribers, and the current print run is 40,000 copies. Your newsletter can pay off for you in many ways beyond just helping you to build your professional practice.

**Q.** I read your book, and you covered all the bases, but I'd like to write, promote, and produce a newsletter for others, rather than start my own newsletter right now.

**A.** Thanks, many readers might feel the same way. This is an alternative for you, but before people will be willing to permit you to produce a newsletter for them, they will likely request some sample copies of other newsletters you have produced; they want proof of your experience in the field. There is no experience better than starting and operating your own newsletter, even if it's only for a year or two.

**Q.** What are the main advantages and opportunities available to me with my own newsletter?

**A.** As I mentioned earlier in the book, you demonstrate your expertise with each issue, and eventually become a specialist in your field. Book publishers might approach you to write a new book in your field; your newsletter is an excellent vehicle to promote your writing and other activities. Newsletter owners have been invited to appear on numerous radio and television talk shows.

**Q.** My newsletter is off to a successful start. When do I begin a second newsletter? I know a friend who has two newsletters going now.

**A.** Slow down. Getting all the necessary elements going smoothly to keep one newsletter running successfully will take all your time and effort in the beginning. Start a second newsletter when your organization can handle the original newsletter satisfactorily.

**Q.** I'm still not sure, even after reading Chapter 2, of the best topic for me. How can I choose?

**A.** I knew this would be a concern for many of my readers. Go to Appendix B of this book, where you will find newsletters on various topics from supervision to printing, to training and education. This Appendix will give you an opportunity to see how other newsletter owners picked a topic and produced a newsletter. You can do it too. Make the effort and give yourself the time necessary to accomplish your goal.

**Q.** Do you have any other comments?

**A.** Yes, Good Luck!

# Appendix B

# The newsletter gallery

Following are samples from several newsletters. Each newsletter owner chose a topic and targeted a specific market. These samples show the wide variety of topics that is available to the prospective owner.

VOLUME 1 NO. 5/SUMMER 1989

# IMPRESSIONS

A newsletter of helpful information and ideas, published by Graymills Corporation, as a service to our customers

## Viscosity & Water Inks

When discussing solvent inks, no one questions the need for viscosity control. But whenever water-based materials are discussed, the question is always asked..."Do we need viscosity control?". Viscosity is one of the key variables in flexo and gravure printing. If you do not have a viscosity maintenance program, you do not have control of a very critical variable. Also, if you're printing water inks on non-absorbent substrate, viscosity control is critical.

Although water inks do not have an evaporation rate as fast as solvent, you do have evaporation. When water inks deteriorate, it happens suddenly. Unlike solvent inks, once water materials have gone "bad", it's virtually impossible to bring them back to a printable state. Therefore, in addition to all the arguments on the benefits of viscosity control for quality and ink mileage, you can save on the cost of waste ink.

In addition, Ph is a factor you will need to control. It is an important part of viscosity maintenance and print quality. Your ink maker will probably recommend a blend that contains some amine

in your viscosity maintenance additions. This should be a carefully measured process and he is best able to instruct you in how this should be done.

Water is cheap, and therefore some press operators work on the theory that if a quart of water is good, a gallon is better. The ink maker blends his ingredients to give you specific printability characteristics. Water inks reduce much more rapidly than solvent type. Too much water can destroy the ink balance causing foaming, along with print quality and drying problems. Be sure your press operators understand the importance of proper water additions.

Viscosity control can be done automatically or by hand with an efflux cup and stop watch. Be sure the cup is clean and undamaged. The watch should be fully wound or the batteries fresh. Train your operators on how you want the readings done so that you get consistency with different operators and shifts. This is critical to uniform readings.

With automatic viscosity controllers, once the operator has set his units, they will continually monitor the running vis-

cosity. As soon as a change takes place, a small amount of "solvent" will be added as soon as a variance is detected. Because the viscosity is being continually monitored, it does not have a chance to vary more than slightly before a correction begins. Also, because the change is very small, print quality is not affected and control is not lost.

So, if you want to print quality... reduced waste...and maximum ink mileage, viscosity control is needed on water materials as much as on solvent type.

## Visgard-4 Reaches European Market!

In March of 1988, Graymills installed a Visgard-4 system on a 6-color Comexi C.I. flexographic press at the Comexi

plant in Girona, Spain. The press and the Visgard-4 were destined for a customer in Denmark. The installation was performed by Ralph Lichtenberger, Graymills Manager of International Development, and Ken Luedtke, Manager, Product Engineering.

The unit, which was equipped with portable stands, solvent supply and Graymills QH53 pumps, ran beautifully in Spain for its test run, then was disassembled and shipped along with the press to Denmark for reassembly.

The Danish printer, which prints

predominantly high quality plastic bags, recently reported that they use the Visgard-4 for their longer runs, and are extremely satisfied with its performance.

Graymills now has Visgard-4 systems operating in English, French, Spanish and German.

| In This Issue.... | |
| --- | --- |
| Efflux Cup Studies | page 2 |
| V-4 Savings Documented | page 3 |
| Visgard Mounting Options | page 4 |

*A newsletter that provides information on printing products and equipment.*

December 1994

# Workskills

**Tips from Boardman Temporary Help Services for Managing Your Work**

## *Management of Your Interruptions at Work*

*S*uccessful people have a common skill which sets them apart from their competition: Full concentration on getting the most important things done for today, without excessive concern about the future or the past. This article will give you some ideas about how you can direct your full concentration toward the most important resource you have in your arsenal: your time.

### Set up the priorities for the day

What do you want to accomplish today? What is the most important thing you can do today?

Alice is a sales representative for a large insurance company. She promised her boss to increase insurance policy sales to engineering and technical employees at the local manufacturing company in her city. Alice will spend the full day trying to get appointments with this special group. This will become her number 1 priority.

Fred is an accounts receivable clerk with a large computer company. His important priority is to work on a large account which is more than 60 days overdue on its invoices. Successful people examine their jobs, determine what important priorities are needed, and work on them daily.

### Deal with your interruptions

Just because you choose your priority carefully and begin it first thing in the morning does not mean yesterday's and tomorrow's priorities will not get in the way of your progress.

DIG A WELL
BEFORE
YOU'RE THIRSTY.

CHINESE PROVERB

In This Issue:

*A practical newsletter on managing human resources today.*

# NESS NEWSLETTER

## SUPERIOR SERVICE IN PROFESSIONAL SECURITY

### WORKPLACE SEARCHES

A major security issue today is the right of an employer to search employee's property or property provided to employees such as desks or lockers. The U.S. Constitution does not protect employees from searches by non-government officials, but common law rights of privacy often gain acceptance by courts in civil suits. The Bureau of National Affairs (BNA) has published guidelines for employers to help protect and preserve the right to search and to assist in defense in the event of a lawsuit.

- When lockers, desks, or offices are assigned, make it clear to the user that the equipment or facility assigned may be searched.

- Where keys are provided to offices or lockers, keep a duplicate set. If employees provide their own locks, require them to provide a key or the combination.

- Establish written policies outlining the circumstances under which searches will be conducted. Publicize these policies to all employees.

- To preserve the right to search at random, conduct random searches periodically. A written policy that is never used is subject to challenge.

- Prohibit or place a limit on the number or type of containers, such as luggage, gym bags, lunch boxes, etc. that an employee can bring on the property.

### SAVINGS BOND PROGRAM

Lil Barnum of the Human Resources Department wishes to remind all of our employees that we have a Savings Bond Program. You can elect to have $5.00 or more deducted from your weekly paycheck. Call our Payroll Department if you wish to participate. We hope you will take advantage of this easy way to put something away for a rainy day.

*A newsletter on professional security.*

QUILL CORPORATION

**VOLUME 1, NUMBER 2**

# NewsClips

*YOUR SOURCE FOR NEWSLETTER ARTICLES CLIP OR COPY AND USE FOR YOUR OWN NEWSLETTER*

*SEE THE LAST PAGE FOR HOW TO USE NEWSCLIPS IN YOUR NEWSLETTER*

## LETTER TO THE EDITORS

"**E**xtra! Extra! Read all about it!" yells the boy on the corner as he holds up a newspaper with a bold headline.

We can all picture this scene from old movies. Unfortunately, as editors we can't physically yell at our potential readers to grab their attention. However, we can use an important tool that has a similar effect: the headline.

Headlines are the most important words on the page. Why? Because they either stop the reader and get him/her to read on, or they don't. Most readers skim reading material and headlines help them select stories to read in-depth.

If you are like me, you can use all the help you can get to improve the headlines in your newsletter. Here are some tips I'd like to share with you on how to write bang-up headlines:

● Use present tense. This gives your headlines a sense of immediacy. Also, write in the active voice and use strong action verbs.

● Be specific and accurate. The headline must summarize the story.

● Don't use commands. People don't respond well to orders.

● Be brief. Don't repeat words, overuse abbreviations or numbers, or use unnecessary words.

● Don't use headlines that are misleading or have double meanings. This confuses your readers.

● Don't use job titles. They clutter up your headlines.

● Avoid bad headline splits. The first line of a multi-line headline should be able to stand alone.

Do you have any other tips on this subject to share with our readers? Or any other issues you'd like us to address in this or other columns for you or your readers? If so, please drop me a line or give me a call. I'd appreciate your input.

*Linda Mimms*

Linda Mimms, Editor

## DOLLARS & SENSE

### Great Customer Service Pays

**D**id you know that it can cost you five times as much to replace a customer as it does to keep one? Or that one dissatisfied customer tells **three times** as many people about his experience than one satisfied customer does?

The message here is that it is less expensive to provide the best customer service you can and therefore maintain new and old customers than it is to provide poor customer service and have to race to replace unhappy customers.

Any organization, large or small, can provide great customer service. All it takes are commitment and adherence to a few basic guidelines. Here's what you need to do:

● Develop a company-wide commitment to customer service, starting from the very top.

● Create appropriate standards and policies that will give your organization a competitive edge.

● Hire, train, manage and infuse in everyone in your organization a commitment to ensure outstanding customer service.

● Choose suppliers that will complement and strengthen your customer service objectives.

● Constantly monitor your customer service efforts to ensure that you are headed in the right direction and that your organization is meeting your customers' expectations.

● Go beyond good customer service by coming up with new ideas to keep improving service.

● Let your current and prospective customers know the kind of service you offer and how it will benefit them.

*A publication for other newsletter owners, which reprints newsletter articles.*

# Communicator

May /June , 1989

*A Newsletter for employees and friends of SMI*                                    *Volume 2, Number 3*

## ANNUAL CLEAN-UP

*Spring has sprung. So have the unsightly views of dead wood, overgrown grass and chipping paint.*

Once again, Joe Cicero invited employees of Systems Management to the annual Spring fix-up, clean-up, paint up picnic outing, which was held Saturday, April 22, 1989. Employees of Systems Management (and a few lucky spouses) all pitched in to make the SMI grounds a much lovelier vision to behold.

The sidewalks and curbs were painted. Dead trees were unnestled and removed from the premises, grass was mowed,the planters were cleaned, and the drives

and parking lots were swept. Not too bad for a day's work.

Of course, the annual riverbank committee was also out in style at the warehouse facility. The river was once again combed for debris, dead trees were removed, and flowers and bushes planted last Spring were pruned.

A very special and warm thanks to all who participated and made our annual clean-up, once again a success.

By the way, the workers were not without reward. They topped off with a picnic and beverages.

Thanks again to the following for their participation:

*Joe and Ginger Cicero,Ralph and Sue Pallerino,Kenny and Cassandra Adamo, Jim Burick,Tom Tinstman, Dale Bonner, Ray Rich, Bill Biddle, Bob and Laurie DiGia,Tim Ryan,Ron Democko,Denny Ross, Don Henderson and Mac Pollard.*

### Inside this Issue

*Spotlite*
*Safety*
*Home Office Profile*
*Operations Changes*
*We Get Letters*
*New Accounts*

*A company-sponsored newsletter for service personnel.*

# FEEDBACK

### The Speech and Hearing Newsletter

A·E·I·O·U

## SPEECH PATHOLOGY, INC.
BARBARA NEWMAN, M.A., C.C.C.-S.P.

Vol. 6
No. 2

2131 Hollywood Blvd., Suite 204
Hollywood, Florida 33020
(305) 922-TALK / 748-7200

*Established since 1974*
Serving Broward, Palm Beach,
and North Dade Counties

**INSIDE**
▸ **Effective Communication**
▸ **Seek Help Early**

Ideas to Educate the Referral Sources, Patients, and Clients of the Speech Pathologist and Audiologist

## Better Hearing and Speech Month Emphasizes Proper Treatment

More than 22 million Americans, 10 percent of the population, have speech, language, or hearing impairments. Communication disorders are the nation's most prevalent handicapping condition. While most of these individuals can be helped by trained professionals, millions often do not realize that help is available or how they can get it.

May is Better Hearing and Speech Month which presents an opportunity for those in need to obtain the help of professionals in the field.

Speech-language pathologists and audiologists are the professionals specifically trained to work with individuals who have communicative disorders in an effort to improve or restore their communication function.

| |
|---|
| Articulation |
| Stuttering |
| Swallowing |
| Language |
| Hearing |
| Voice |

The earlier a problem is diagnosed and treatment begins, the better the chances for improvement, and for the afflicted person to be able to lead a normal, productive life. It is never too late to seek help. Mrs. Annie Glenn, the wife of U.S. Senator John Glenn of Ohio, finally overcame stuttering while in her fifties with the help of a speech-language pathologist.

We urge anyone who suffers from a speech, language, voice, swallowing, or hearing disorder to learn more about it and to seek professional help.

### Communication Disorders May be Related To:

- Stroke
- Head Injury
- Cancer
- Cerebral Palsy
- Cleft Palate
- Functional Problem
- Environmental Problem
- Birth Defects
- Accent

## Signaling Devices for Hearing Impaired

*by Diane L. Castle, Ph.D.*
*Reprinted with permission from*
*Alexander Graham Bell Association for*
*the Deaf. Washington, D.C.*

In recent years, people have begun to recognize the need for special signaling devices for hearing-impaired persons. Movie and television star Nanette Fabray, who was severely hearing impaired for many years due to otosclerosis, believes strongly in the importance of signaling devices.

"One of my personal projects is to get all major hotels to have some kind of wake-up device for a deaf person...(and) some kind of emergency lights so a deaf person knows if something has gone wrong."

Signaling devices are used to warn people when there is an important sound nearby. There are two ways for equipment to signal: with **light** or with **vibration**.

One device sometimes can be used as a signaler for different sounds. Devices with **microphones** will be sensitive to sounds such as the doorbell, voices, a baby crying, a dog barking, the telephone, TV or radio, and smoke or burglar alarms. When using this kind of device,

*continued on page 2*

*A newsletter for patients of speech pathologists and audiologists.*

Vol. II, No. 1, January-February 1990

# BACK COUNTRY HOMEWORKERS● EXCHANGE

Dear Readers,

Have you ever heard that commercial,

> "I can bring home the bacon
> fry it up in the pan
> and never ever let you forget you're a man
> cause I'm a WOOOO-MAN..."

I'll bet you $50 a man conceived that commercial, strip-tease music and all. Probably was a man who came up with the phrase "Super-Mom," too; trying to make it all sound heroic and glorious. Well believe me honey, by the time I'm done bringin that bacon home and fryin it all up, I could care less whether you're a man or not - I'm goin to sleep!

Not that any of this is the fault of our men. They're as bewildered by it all as we are; they just aren't all that much help. The unfortunate side of the industrial revolution is that it separated our work from the rest of our lives. Now astronomical housing prices as well as universal, unrelenting pressure from our surroundings to consume have created an economy in which most women have go out to work, even those who feel that homemaking and mothering are more important.

"Women Working Home" by Marion Behr and Wendy Lazar (and a host of other home-working contributors) is billed as "The Homebased Business Guide and Directory." I have the second edition (copyright 1983, WWH Press, New Jersey) and it is truly the best compilation of solid information and advice from successful homeworking women I have ever laid my hands on. On the first page of the

introduction is a quote that, for me, really says it all:

> "Working from home is the most practical, sensible, and personally rewarding way of life for women today. Those of us who really want to have some sort of career or identity beyond that of housewife/mother and yet do not want to abandon that role and those responsibilities, really have no other good alternative."

Since first publishing "Back country Homemakers' Exchange" nearly one year ago, without fail my most enthusiastic feedback, from women I've felt were really reaching out, has been from homeworking women. That is why, beginning with this issue, "Back country Homemakers' Exchange" has become "Back country Homeworkers' Exchange," with a tighter focus on the interests and needs of rural homeworkers.

Let us know how we do! And Best of Luck to us all.

Best regards,

*Kyle*

Kyle Staples
Editor

*A newsletter for home-based business people.*

# WELLSPRING

*...the water that I shall give will turn into a spring inside you, welling up to eternal life*

John 4:14

| VOLUME VI   NUMBER 1 | WINTER 1988 | OFFICE OF SPIRITUAL DEVELOPMENT |

## A Word from the Director

**Rev. John Dooher, Director**
**Office of Spiritual Development**

One of the major themes of Pope John Paul II's pastoral visit to the United States was the universal call to holiness and the importance of prayer for the spiritual life. As the Office of Spiritual Development enters its second decade, we hear the words of our Holy Father as an affirmation of all that has been accomplished over the past ten years and as a continuing challenge for the future.

In this issue of Wellspring, we have invited the reflection of a few people who have assisted the work of spiritual development over the years. However, they represent a much larger number of faithful, dedicated priests, religious, lay men and lay women who have shared their faith with tens of thousands of parishioners throughout the archdiocese. We look back with gratitude to

God for all our speakers who have volunteered their time and talent, for the thousands of laity who have served their parishes as members of parish spiritual development advisory boards and for the spiritual leadership of so many priests.

The centrality of prayer in responding to the call to holiness has been a hallmark of the Initial Retreats, Evenings of Prayer, Parish Missions and Further Evangelization aspects of this apostolate. As we look forward, the words of our Holy Father challenge all those engaged in the spiritual development program: "If you really wish to follow Christ, if you want your love for him to grow and last, then you must be faithful in prayer. It is the key to the vitality of your life in Christ."

*A religious publication about social and renewal programs.*

# BOOK MARKETING UPDATE

Ad-Lib Publicati⬚⬚⬚⬚⬚⬚ ⬚2, Fairfield, IA 52556-1102

November / December 1990 — Issue #24          ISSN 0891-8813          Subscription: $48.00 per year

## The Making of a Best-Seller

### What's a Best-Seller?

While a best-seller is often defined by the lists maintained by the *New York Times* or *Publisher Weekly*, these lists are not — by any means — the only way to measure success. Indeed, these lists are questionable. Among other things, they clearly favor the heavily promoted books published by the big New York publishers.

For example, in compiling its list, the *New York Times* submits a list of 36 titles to about 3,000 bookstores across the country and asks those bookstores to fill in the number of copies of each book they sold that week. If your book is not on that list of 36 titles, it will not get on that week's best-seller list — even if your book outsold every other book in the country. Well, it does have a slim chance, because the *Times* does leave a blank space where booksellers can enter the names of other titles which sold well in their stores, but few bookstores bother to note the sales of unlisted titles. As one bookstore polled by the *Times* noted, "You can be assured that no book in that space ever makes the best-seller list."

### How to Make the Times List

Given the obstacles to making the major best-seller lists, it is not impossible. Recently, for example, Prelude Press promoted Peter McWilliams's new book, *Life 101* to the top ten of all the major best-seller lists. How did they do it? Here are a few of the things they did:

- First, they planned far in advance of the publication date.

- Second, they began advertising in the major trade magazines, *Publishers Weekly* and *American Bookseller*, months before the book came out. These ads were full page black and white ads extolling the virtues of the upcoming book and the author's track record on previous books.

- They sent out advance review copies to a targeted list of major book media (newspapers, magazines, TV shows, etc.)

- For the three weeks prior to publication date and the five weeks after, they sent out at least one news release each week. Each news release built upon the other — and announced the success the book had thus far enjoyed (including any regional best-seller lists it had made).

In all, Prelude spent about $10,000 in trade advertising and another $10,000 in its publicity campaign to promote the book. That works out to about $2.00 per copy for their initial print run of 10,000 copies. Of course, because the campaign worked (the book got as high as #3 on the *Times* list), they could amortize the cost of the campaign over a greater number of books.

### Other Best-Seller Lists

While the *Times* and *PW* list are the most influential lists, your book has many opportunities to become a certified best-seller. Here are just a few of the opportunities:

- **Wholesaler best-seller lists** — Many wholesalers maintain best-seller lists, including Ingram (with best-seller lists for computer books, children's books, science fiction, cookbooks, etc.), Inland (with its annual *Poetry Checklist* of the top 50 poetry books), New Leaf with its top 50 best-selling books in four catagories (conscious living, metaphysical, wellness, and young readers), and so on.

  Ad-Lib's *Mail Order Selling Made Easier* made Quality Book's Small Press Top 40 in both June and August of this year!

- **Magazine best-seller lists** — The *Voice Literary Supplement, Lambda Rising Book Report, Locus,* and *Bloomsbury Review* (among others) all feature best-seller lists compiled from independent and specialized booksellers around the country.

  Each issue of the *Library Journal* features a list of books most in demand by librarians (as reported by Baker & Taylor).

- **Speciality best-seller lists** — The Christian Booksellers Association and Spring Arbor Distributors compile a monthly list of the top 20 Christian clothbound, paperback, and children's best-sellers.

  The *Chronicle of Higher Education* compiles a list of the best-selling trade books in college bookstores (based on sales in 150 such stores).

When your books make one of these lists, don't hesitate to let other people know, especially your distributor, your sales reps, major wholesalers, key bookstore accounts, and appropriate media. When you go back to reprint the book, add a tagline on your cover announcing that the book is a best-seller.

*A comprehensive bi-monthly newsletter on marketing books.*

# Appendix C

# Checklist for starting a home-based newsletter

Set up a schedule for yourself. Commit to get the tasks outlined below done by a specific date, and check off each task as you accomplish it.

| Date | ✔ | |
|------|---|---|
| _____ | ____ | 1. Set up a room or a special area to write |
| _____ | ____ | 2. Select a newsletter subject |
| _____ | ____ | 3. Research your topic according to current competition |
| _____ | ____ | 4. Select a target market |
| _____ | ____ | 5. Choose a name and subtitle |
| _____ | ____ | 6. Do a mission statement and a golden contract |

| Date | ✔ | |
|------|---|---|
| _____ | ___ | 7. Select content to build a winning newsletter |
| _____ | ___ | 8. Select and write articles that appeal to your market |
| _____ | ___ | 9. Edit for clarity and focus |
| _____ | ___ | 10. Proofread your final copy |
| _____ | ___ | 11. Design your newsletter |
| _____ | ___ | 12. Prepare and schedule your quality printing |
| _____ | ___ | 13. Mail out your newsletter |
| _____ | ___ | 14. Market your newsletter all year long |
| _____ | ___ | 15. Use powerful public relations techniques |
| _____ | ___ | 16. Manage your newsletter business |
| _____ | ___ | 17. Congratulations, keep up the good work |

# Index

Index note: An *f.* after a page number refers to a figure.

## About the Author

William J. Bond is a newsletter publisher, teacher, writer, and consultant. He is the author of the best-selling *Home-Based Mail Order: A Success Guide for Entrepreneurs.* Mr. Bond is a frequent writer on the subject of business success, and appears on many radio and television shows. He is also the founder of a very popular seminar on the subject of newsletter publishing.